Frontier Military Series
XIV

Ulysses S. Grant, age 27 years, in 1849.
This is the last known photogaph of Grant
prior to the Civil War.
Courtesy, Ohio Historical Society

The Trial of
U.S. Grant

The Pacific Coast Years
1852-1854

by
Charles G. Ellington

with a Foreword by
John Y. Simon

THE ARTHUR H. CLARK COMPANY
Glendale, California   1987

LIBRARY OF CONGRESS CATALOG CARD NUMBER 86-50835
ISBN 0-87062-169-6

Library of Congress Cataloging-in-Publication Data

Ellington, Charles G.
   The trial of U.S. Grant.

   (Frontier military series ; 14)
   Bibliography: p.
   Includes index.
   1. Grant, Ulysses S. (Ulysses Simpson), 1822-1885.
2. Presidents—United States—Biography. 3. Generals—
United States—Biography. 4. United States. Army—
Biography. 5. Frontier and pioneer life—California.
I. Title. II. Series.
E672.E45 1986   973.8'2'0924   86-50835
ISBN 0-87062-169-6

For Nancy,
with love

Contents

Illustrations

Preface

In the mid-1970s I began to study the life of Ulysses S. Grant. I soon found that the stereotyped image I had formed earlier was far off the mark. Then when I learned that Grant had been on the Pacific Coast during early pioneer days, an area where I lived and worked, I was hooked.

I spent the next decade (not full-time, of course) following Grant's trail in California, Washington and Oregon. I visited every place he did, walked in his footsteps, and attempted to see this vibrant land through his eyes. The only piece of the story I could not duplicate was his crossing of the Isthmus of Panama. But I did the next best thing. I talked with the honored California historian, John Haskell Kemble, who wrote his dissertation on the Panama crossing in the 1930s, after poking around the region invaded by the canal. Dr. Kemble, now retired as head of the history department at Pomona College, is the acknowledged expert on the Panama crossing, and he shared with me his enthusiasm and the spirit of those days.

My search led me to the "headquarters" of Grant scholarship at Southern Illinois University in Carbondale. There, under the leadership of the foremost Grant scholar, John Y. Simon, the definitive work on Ulysses Grant has taken place. To my eternal gratitude this group accepted me. I became an active director of the U. S. Grant Association, and through them have been introduced to every facet of Grant's life. A highpoint of this pleasurable experience came in 1985 when I was asked to preside in the Rotunda of the U. S. Capitol at the ceremony marking the 100th anniversary of Grant's death. John Simon, Ralph Newman, David Wilson, Sue Dotson and others of the Grant Association, are my dear friends and have taught me much. My fellow director, E. B. "Pete" Long, before his untimely death, read portions of this manuscript and was excited by what I was trying to do. I am sorry he cannot ascertain if I approached his high expectations.

In completing my research, and at every point thereafter, I had the unselfish help of my comrade, Curtis W. Tarr. Dr. Tarr, now dean of the Johnson Graduate School of Management at Cornell University, has been my close friend since 1944 when we shared the rigors of World War II. Our companionship has lasted from the snows of Bastogne, to Harvard's ivy-covered bricks, Pentagon gray walls, and the warmer climes of his native California. I owe much to this distinguished American, and not just because he read every word of this book and commented constructively on my efforts.

As I followed Grant's life on the West Coast I studied in almost one hundred libraries, historical societies, and museums in seven states and the District of Columbia. From the major institutions of the Huntington Library, the National Archives, and the Bancroft Library at the University of California, Berkeley to smaller collections at Yreka, California, Klamath Falls, Oregon, and Webster Groves, Missouri, I pursued my objective to learn about U. S. Grant. I have been aided at every turn by patient librarians, enthusiastic antiquarians, and selfless history buffs. Literally, scores of individuals have contributed to this book. I can say truthfully that without exception these fine men and women went out of their way to help me. It is a shame that sheer numbers make it impossible to acknowledge their help further. But they know who they are and they will know of my warm gratitude.

Members of the Grant family provided inspiration and background. Edith Grant Griffiths, the General's great-granddaughter, introduced me to the family's dignified lifestyle. U. S. Grant IV, a retired professor in Los Angeles, forcefully reminded me of the straightforward courage of his famous grandfather when he wrote to cancel an interview because "I am sick in bed with what may well be my terminal illness." And Chapman Grant, over 90 and the last surviving grandchild of the General, became my friend — for a time — and entertained me with rollicking tales of his grandmother Julia's visits to San Diego when Chapman was a child.

Two other good friends played an important role in the completion of this work. Dorothy Lindberg and Mickey Eppard volunteered their encouragement. Mickey in the early days and Dorothy during the past five years cheerfully pushed me along and have my sincere thanks.

The Henry E. Huntington Library, for years my neighbor in San Marino, California, provided desk space, friendly surroundings and staff, an unbelievable breadth of source material, and Ray Allen Billington. Dr. Billington, before he died, became interested in my topic and passed his 'helpful comments along.

My colleagues in the Office of the Secretary of Defense made it possible for me to schedule my time off to the best advantage of my research and helped find information that exists only in the nation's Capital. Their help is gratefully acknowledged.

It is necessary to record that with all the help from these distinguished personages who took time to advise me, and the many others who contributed, I am accountable alone for any mistakes in judgement or of fact in this book. Written history is never completely the work of one individual. Usually there are too many ghosts of times past, too many scholars who have peered into each corner for any writer to claim exclusiveness. I had much assistance in this work, though I can claim rightly that it is mine.

The Civil War was the watershed event of American history. The "ordeal of the Union" has fascinated Americans as a dramatic touchstone of our national life. It is fitting therefore to learn more about the major actors in that drama. Ulysses Grant was a central character in the story. If we know more about Grant and his beginnings, we shall understand more about ourselves as Americans.

Finally, I thank my wife Nancy Gordon Perry Ellington for her love and support, without which this modest book would have no meaning for me.

Charles G. Ellington
Bellevue, Washington
May, 1986

Foreword

At Grant's Tomb on Memorial Day, 1908, Secretary of War William Howard Taft spoke glowingly of Grant's character and achievements, contrasting the latter with early adversity. His initial military career was routine, Taft suggested, "but in 1854 he resigned from the Army because he had to. He had yielded to the weakness of a taste for strong drink, and rather than be court-martialed he left the Army." He returned to his family "a disheartened man," to face new adversities for seven years before the Civil War, but nonetheless "overcame in a great measure his weakness for strong drink."

Already on his way to the Republican nomination for president as Theodore Roosevelt's hand-picked successor, Taft might have known that his statements would receive careful attention, but he appeared unprepared for a barrage of criticism of his generous tribute to Grant, all based on the issue of whether Grant drank to excess on the Pacific Coast. Taft reminded critics that his father had served in Grant's Cabinet and had raised his children with an "intense reverence" for Grant, that the younger Taft had based his statements on Hamlin Garland's biography of Grant and had supposed his statements accurate.

Garland had interviewed many surviving friends and acquaintances of Grant for this biography, that first appeared serially in *McClure's Magazine,* then in book form in 1898. Thirty years earlier, however, Albert D. Richardson, a newspaper correspondent, who had known Grant in the field and had also interviewed numerous people, had published *A Personal History of U. S. Grant,* an adulatory biography designed for consumption during the presidential election of 1868, in which he had told essentially the same story of Grant's weakness for liquor leading to his resignation from the army. In his 1908 speech, not expected to be based on original research, Taft had hardly broken new ground or given voice to mere rumor.

Taft was neither the first nor last to stumble over a familiar feature of American folklore: the alleged fact that Grant's excessive drinking caused his resignation from the army. Indeed, Taft was embarrassed by newspaper stories that made use of materials in War Department files to show the absence of any documentary evidence for a forced resignation. Whatever the truth of the matter, the story of a forced resignation had flourished among army officers after 1854 so vigorously that eight years later one professional soldier, Major General Henry W. Halleck telegraphed to Major General George B. McClellan that "a rumor has just reached me that since the taking of Fort Donelson General Grant has resumed his former bad habits." Halleck gave no further details on the "habits," quite unnecessary when one professional communicated with another. Since Grant was not drinking heavily after the battle of Fort Donelson, a period when he was under close scrutiny by the officers and men of his command, and had incurred the displeasure of Halleck through communications deficiencies that lay beyond his control, the validity of such army gossip for any period of his life must be carefully examined. This is a major achievement of *The Trial of U. S. Grant.*

As Charles G. Ellington amply demonstrates in his important study of Grant's two-year tour of duty on the Pacific Coast, much that happened in the period 1852-54 remains obscure, including the combination of factors impelling Grant's resignation from the army. Nonetheless, Ellington recognizes that these years of forced separation from his family, assignments to routine duties, economic adversity, ill health, and career frustration played a major role in shaping an extraordinary American. Never before have these years been separated from the remainder of Grant biography to receive such close scrutiny, one that combines Grant scholarship with careful attention to local Pacific Coast history and a personal knowledge of the terrain.

In later years as well, Grant demonstrated ability to learn from adversity. As commander, he rebounded from the error of allowing his troops to be surprised on the first day of the battle of Shiloh, and from the folly of direct assault on entrenchments at Vicksburg and Cold Harbor. At the end of his life, the victim of a Wall Street swindle and dying of cancer, he roused unexpected reserves of inner strength to write his *Memoirs,* both a means to provide for his family and to present a record of his military career in the form of a literary classic.

Before Grant was assigned to the Pacific Coast in 1852,

his life and career had possessed little of the extraordinary, nothing to suggest that he was anyone more than a small-town Ohioan who had the good fortune to receive an appointment to the United States Military Academy and sufficient ability to perform creditably as a junior officer. In the Mexican War, his superiors noted his bravery and skill, but in no special manner, and he had been placed in a position where his role was determined by his training and the example of his peers.

On the Pacific Coast, he encountered his first experience of true solitude. The few friends he found, within and outside the army, gave him little opportunity to follow the example of others. Life at Fort Vancouver, even more at Fort Humboldt, took on the attributes of an ordeal. As he found himself increasingly "forsaken," deprived of family in effect by the slowness of the mails and of friends by assignment to Fort Humboldt, he drew on his own resources and plotted his own course, a foreshadowing of the isolation of top command during the Civil War. During years of virtual exile, he developed the strength of character that enabled him to persevere through the seven years of adversity that lay ahead: farming at Hardscrabble in St. Louis County and seeing his efforts come to naught during the panic of 1857, fruitlessly searching for a job in the city of St. Louis, finally accepting his father's offer of a clerkship in the family leather store in Galena, Illinois, where he was virtually the employee of a brother thirteen years younger.

In August, 1861, a former army captain living in Galena, who had briefly served as aide to Governor Richard Yates of Illinois during the early days of the Civil

War, and had been appointed by the governor colonel of an unusually disorderly Illinois regiment, was unexpectedly appointed a brigadier general by President Abraham Lincoln, largely through the influence of Congressman Elihu B. Washburne of Galena, a powerful Republican who had no better qualified constituent to offer for the honor. At the time of the appointment, Grant led his regiment in Missouri but had yet to encounter the enemy. In retrospect, Grant may appear to have been an officer untested for the responsibilities of command. As Ellington demonstrates, however, Grant had already been tested nearly a decade earlier.

John Y. Simon
Executive Director
Ulysses S. Grant Association

Carbondale, Illinois
April, 1986

GUARD HOUSE
BUILT IN 1872

This is the third guard house built on the former arsenal grounds. It is pointed out primarily because the first guard house, built in 1852, was the setting of the trial of Second Lieutenant Ulysses S. Grant, later President of the United States, charged with a minor infraction of military regulations. The rear portion of the building housed the military fire equipment.

BENICIA INDUSTRIES, INC.

Historical Marker at the Benicia Arsenal.
Photo by the author at Benicia, California.

Chapter I

Brevet Captain Grant

The white-framed historical marker stood before the restored guard house at the old Benicia, California Army Arsenal. The Arsenal is now a humming industrial park and port with warehouses, manufacturing plants, and hundreds of Japanese automobiles awaiting distribution throughout the West.

In stark, simple words the marker reported that the Arsenal's "first guard house built in 1852 was the setting of the trial of Second Lieutenant Ulysses S. Grant later President of the United States charged with a minor infraction of military regulations." Local lore had it that the young lieutenant was drunk, tried by a military court, and jailed overnight.

Something about that story was bothersome, yet few seemed knowledgeable about Grant being in California. Further, it was not widely known that Grant had been on trial or that key events in his life took place on the West Coast. This puzzling footnote of history began an investigation that provided an insight into the life of an unusual American.

The facts relating to Grant's West Coast experiences are uncomplicated. From mid-1852 to the summer of 1854 Captain Ulysses S. Grant, then in his early thirties, was stationed in California, Oregon, and Washington. Captain Grant served on the Pacific West Coast for these two years without his beloved wife Julia and his two young sons, one of whom he had never seen.

Grant graduated from West Point in 1843 and had been one of the many young Academy officers who fought in the Mexican War, an illustrious group that included R. E. Lee, James Longstreet, and Thomas Jackson. "Captain Sam," as he was called by his friends, was assigned to routine duties on the West Coast, pursued civilian investments as others did, made little professional progress, and was sometimes not comfortable with his commanding officer. In 1854 when he resigned from the army that he had served loyally throughout his adult life, Grant looked forward to becoming a prosperous Missouri farmer within ten years. This was not to be. During those ten years he was less than successful as a farmer, a salesman, and a clerk. Yet at the end of that time, U. S. Grant — next to the soon-to-be martyred President — was the most popular, most revered American and became the highest ranking officer in the army. What happened to Grant on the West Coast? Why was he tried, and what was the verdict?

U. S. Grant's time on the Pacific Coast seemed worth researching and reporting. The West Coast was where he suffered, where he plunged to the depths of discouragement, where he gave up on the army and it on him. The story of young Sam Grant's time on the Pacific Coast in the early 1850s was not so much a story of failure or disappointment as it was the continuing strict apprenticeship that developed the character of the man who literally saved the American nation.

Brevet Captain Grant, like others who would become

national figures, distinguished himself in the battle fires of the Mexican conflict. He thought that war the most disgraceful his country had ever fought, yet Grant had passed well the test of combat. Now, at age 31, the young career officer was posted to his second "overseas" assignment.

Into the early years of marriage that truly was heaven blessed, with a fine strapping baby boy, Grant was ordered to his country's farthest frontier, the Pacific Coast, at a time when he was bored by the routine of army life. Gold, Indians, scrambling settlers, scenic grandeur, a new society bursting at the seams, all lay before him. But as the sensible, careful family man he had grown to be, Grant knew he would have to go alone, at least until he could prepare properly for his growing family. Julia was seven months pregnant when Grant's orders arrived.

The young officer's journey took him across the Isthmus of Panama, a harrowing trip, through the "wonderland" of a booming San Francisco, up the broad Columbia River where the army had built its most picturesque western post, and finally south again to a shabby, new outpost dominated by gigantic redwoods and plagued by overcast and repetitious days. There was a trial, but it was far different than the marker at Benicia would lead one to believe. The story ended with the lonely homesick soldier's resignation from the army and his determination to turn to civilian pursuits, never again to be separated long from his beloved wife and children.

With the exception of the Panama crossing, Grant's steps in the West were retraced by the author. Skipping rocks at the Stanislaus River ferry site, viewing the valley of Mexico, listening to the sounds of San Francisco, wondering at the immortality of the giant trees, being awestruck by towering Mount Hood, trudging the road from Benicia to the Arsenal gates, exploring hardscrabble mining towns, my aim was to reconstruct Grant's moves and moods.

Bruce Catton expressed the objective so well: "I hope that I have managed to present Grant as the genuinely great, deeply appealing American he really was... He was both a completely representative American and an extremely unusual one..."[1]

Hiram Ulysses Grant was born in a two-room cottage at Point Pleasant, Clermont County, Ohio, a stone's throw from the Ohio River, on April 27, 1822. He went to school in nearby Georgetown and, except for a sweet disposition, a knack with horses, an early developed sense of direction and practical geography, he was not a great deal different than his southern Ohio contemporaries.

Grant was a spunky youngster, wise for his years, who listened to the world and had a boldness, for his age, to strike out on his own. He was loved but not coddled by his mother. The lad was a little in awe of his father who was an active businessman, politician, and promoter.

"Ulys," as his mother sometimes called him, left Ohio in 1839 to enroll in the Military Academy at West Point. His father, seeing a way to provide a good education cheaply, thought his son's doing so was a good idea. Later Grant, who was not interested in a military career, said if his father thought it a good idea perhaps he did too.

Grant's time at West Point went swiftly. He was unexcelled in horsemanship, did well in mathematics, but poorly in French. He was graduated 21 out of 39 in the

---

[1]Bruce Catton, *Grant Moves South* (Boston, 1960), letter to his editor quoted on the dust jacket.

class of 1843 and had his name changed to Ulysses S. Grant. Following the Mexican War Grant married a southern belle, Julia Dent, and began the uninspiring career of a peacetime quartermaster officer in the 4th Infantry Regiment of the United States Army.

With some outstanding exceptions, that shall be noted, most Grant biographers have given short shrift to his time on the Pacific Coast. Typical of this coverage in the rash of Grant books that appeared after the Civil War, are these lines from Charles A. Phelps' lengthy work published in 1868.

> At the close of the Mexican War, Capt. Grant returned to the United States and was subsequently stationed on the Canadian frontier, in California, and in Oregon. But garrison life in that lonely region offered no opportunities of usefulness to himself or others. His years were wasting away in the small duties of an outpost; and as the country was at peace, and had no special need of military service from him, he determined to resign his commission, which he did in July, 1854.[2]

There is much more to the West Coast story than that! But before dealing with those facts in detail, a more general perspective of Grant, the man, and Grant the public servant, must be considered. Perhaps two of these, initially, deserve comment: his reputation as a drinking man and his record as a president.

There seems little doubt that prior to the Civil War, and on occasions during that conflict, Grant drank. But there is solid evidence that as commanding general, President, and after his tenure in high office, he did not overindulge. Indeed, he drank only sparingly of table wines and ale during his later years. His earlier reputation, however, hung as a cloud over him. No

---

[2]Charles A. Phelps, *General Ulysses S. Grant* (Boston, 1868), p. 11.

...ount of Ulysses Grant's life can dodge this subject. Concerning his presidency, historians often minimized the high esteem in which he was held by his contemporaries. His virtues of fortitude, trust, patience, loyalty, resolution, self-control, and kindness, in some ways became liabilities to him as a politician.[3] The most unmilitary general became a most unpolitical president.[4]

During Grant's first term as president the 15th Amendment to the Constitution was adopted with his full support. This provided that suffrage should not be restricted on account of color or previous condition of servitude. Thus the last slaveholder to serve as president continued to do his part to end the evil practice. His administration is credited with settling several serious controversies with Great Britain including the bitter question of damages inflicted upon the United States by Confederate warships built and equipped in England.

Grant favored the annexation of the Dominican Republic, and in the last years of his life he still thought doing so would have settled some of the Caribbean problems that continue to plague us. He alleviated the restrictive reconstruction laws that hamstrung the South. He pushed for the Amnesty Act restoring civil rights to most southerners.

As early as 1870 President Grant recommended measures of civil service reform and appointed the first Civil Service Commission. In his second term he vetoed a ruinous bill that would have debased the currency indefinitely by inflation. And his advocacy of the "Specie Resumption Act" was a credit to his term.

---

[3] Robert H. Keller, Jr. *American Protestantism and United States Indian Policy 1869-82* (Lincoln, 1982), p. 26.
[4] Thomas M. Pitkin, *The Captain Departs* (Carbondale, 1973), p. xiii.

Grant's Indian policy deserved more credit than it received for he brought humanity and leadership to Indian affairs. President Grant's policy of peace "cost less than war, it protected settlers better than war, it eased railroads through Indian country without conflict, it stopped extermination, and it was just."[5] As he demonstrated earlier for the Mexicans, Grant had a great sympathy for the Indians. His exposure to them on the West Coast convinced him that the basic cause of the Indian problem was the white man. "It is really my opinion that the whole race would be harmless and peaceable if they were not put upon by the whites."[6]

Whenever, as President, he did anything wise it had the look of a happy accident. Many thought him incredibly naive. A famous contemporary wrote, "He had no idea of what it meant to be President . . . Grant was the incurable sucker. He easily fell victim to trickery and allowed [others] to betray him into compromising his office because he could not believe such [dishonest] people existed."[7]

But what was Brevet Captain Grant really like? That is the core of this narrative, to report on Grant in his early thirties between 1852-1854. No living person knew then what he was to become or the characteristics with which succeeding generations would credit him. Could anyone have known the discouraged captain would become the first four-star general in the United States Army, the first President to have graduated from West Point, and, literally, first in the hearts of his countrymen?

[5]Keller, *op. cit.*, p. 26.

[6]John Y. Simon, ed., *The Papers of Ulysses S. Grant*, Vol. 1 (Carbondale, 1967), p. 296. (Cited hereafter as Grant, *Papers.*)

[7]Edmund Wilson, *Patriotic Gore: Studies in the Literature of the American Civil War* (New York, 1962), pp. 164-67.

It would be too easy to suggest that character strengths were there in a young man and say, "Grant was destined for greatness ánd you could tell it even then." It is obviously true, however, that what he was at Vicksburg and at the White House derived from experience and character formed during his early years.

Grant, in his youth, was a short, slight, determined-looking man. He had soft "Ohio River accents" and dark gray eyes. All in all, he was a quiet person, but friendly enough when one knew him. He had a straightforward, no-nonsense approach, and Julia said he was the handsomest man she ever saw. Ulysses Grant had an open face not given to smirking or smiling. One can see his attractive features in early pictures, and later, the strength and compassion in the remarkable portraits taken at various times during the Civil War.

Grant had a stubborn side; easily recognized as a steadfast rather than a nervous or flighty man. Lloyd Lewis, that talented newspaper man turned biographer, thought Grant in the Civil War was "ordinary looking — like Truman he looked like Mr. America. Railroad conductors, ticket agents, hotel baggagemen, clerks, *always* failed to recognize him."[8]

Some have recorded that Grant was untidy in his dress. Never a dandy or a fashion plate, he was really unconcerned with his appearance. Except for his West Point days and his visits home during that time, it never occurred to him to spruce up in order to gain approval from those around him.

Major General Frederick Dent Grant, the oldest of U. S. Grant's four children, always regretted he did not write a biography of his father. (Fred Grant's son U. S.

---

[8]Lloyd Lewis, *Letters from Lloyd Lewis* (Boston, 1950), p. 51.

Grant 3rd, did.) But he recorded memories of his father in speeches, articles and interviews. One of his most interesting reminiscences was "My Father As I Knew Him," first published in the *New York World Sunday Magazine,* April 23, 1897. While one would not expect derogatory statements from a loving son who shared closely much of his father's life, Fred Grant's testimony helps us to understand the impression he made upon his family.

> [My father] was a plain, dignified, undemonstrative man, with a quiet, self-controlled manner which never left him, showing a consideration in all his actions and words toward others...
>
> Our father's decision in any matter was absolutely final... he was very careful about making a promise, but he never broke one after making it... In the evenings [he] would read aloud to the family... He seemed especially fond of Dickens' works... I never heard him use a profane word. He never told, or listened to, a vulgar or improper story... he considered them out of place even among men. He was a sensitive and retiring man, but behind his modesty was a fair estimate of his own worth. He tolerated no disrespect and was most determined.
>
> [He] had quite a sense of humor, and was fond of illustrating his opinions with apt stories and anecdotes. He rarely laughed aloud, but his eyes would twinkle... and occasionally... he would utter a gentle laugh. As honors crowded upon him they wrought no change in him. As the president, he was the same sensitive, modest, retiring and considerate gentleman that he had been when a young officer, a farmer... and a merchant...
>
> In battle I have seen him turn hurriedly from the sight of blood, and look pale and distressed when others were injured. At Shiloh... he remained out in the rain all night long rather than accept the shelter which the hospital afforded... [He] endured his own suffering without a murmur... my admiration for him is more because of the fortitude with which he bore his own mental and physical sufferings.
>
> His consideration for others... outweighed all thought of

self... He never knowingly said or did a thing which would wound the sensitive feelings of others.[9]

To understand Grant, one must understand his background. He was a son of the frontier — basically home-spun, reared with the old-fashioned virtues of self-reliance and common sense. He was a small town boy, but he was a lad of vision. Grant, like earlier frontiersmen and their offspring, had an inborn restlessness, wanting to move on to see the other side of the hill. His biographers tell of him always moving, always traveling, never wanting to retrace his steps.

He was neither a slow thinker, nor fast and brilliant in his responses. But Grant had the capacity of massive concentration. One of his West Coast problems was that he concentrated too heavily on his loneliness.

Grant was the kind of person one might easily underestimate, principally because he looked and "projected" as he did. He was easy to talk to, a good listener, and always seemed to have a calm, if slightly melancholy air about him. Later, William Tecumseh Sherman saw him as a simple but powerful person.

Grant believed that getting on with the job was the only way. Even as a student he did not loll around but pitched in and gave his courses his best effort every time. He had a dry wit, but was not a kidder; he was not garrulous outside his family circle. When President Lincoln first met him, he reportedly described Grant as "the quietest little fella you ever did see."

Grant's command of the language was good, but not scholarly; his slightly high-pitched voice could be heard

---

[9]Ulysses S. Grant Assoc. *Newsletter*, Carbondale, Illinois (Apr. 1969), (cited hereafter as *Grant Assoc. Newsletter*).

and commanded attention. He did not curse — "confound it," was as strong as he went, and his spelling was awesome. Yet his *Memoirs* are considered by historians as the finest written by a military figure since Caesar.

John Y. Simon, Professor of American History at Southern Illinois University at Carbondale, Executive Director of the Ulysses S. Grant Association, Editor of the projected twenty-five volume *Papers of U. S. Grant,* and author of articles and books about Grant and his family, has studied, and "lived" with Ulysses Grant for twenty-two years. Dr. Simon knows Grant better than any other living person.

In late September 1981, in Arlington, Virginia, the author talked with John Simon about Grant's pre-Civil War experiences and the person he was. That conversation which lasted several hours is summarized below.[10]

The first thing that comes to mind in introducing Brevet Capt. Grant is that description by his future sister-in-law . . . "as pretty as a doll." He was slight and thin and always worried about the possibility of tuberculosis which did, in fact, carry off a brother and a sister. Apparently there was a tendency toward it in his family.

In many ways Grant was a very ordinary looking young man and probably in terms of his social relationships, unremarkable to those who knew him casually. In later years, everybody would say "I always had Grant marked out as a special man," but they never wrote it down at the time and there is no evidence to make those people gifted with anything except hindsight on

[10]Conversation with Dr. John Y. Simon, Sept. 1981, Arlington, Virg.

this. He was a very decent man. One of the keys to his whole character is the word "Victorian"... his Victorian outlook in morals, in his general perspective, in his speech, eating habits and for that matter, perhaps even drinking habits.

Grant was a sensitive young man with more literary interests than most of the officers of that time. Probably one of the few cadets who made his peace with West Point because it had a decent library where he could read novels. There is very little evidence that he read anything else. He made a point of saying that he only read over his lessons once and his record in French would suggest that maybe he had not read those lessons even once.

He had an aptitude for mathematics which must have been remarkable, because with a relatively mediocre academic record, he was considered as a potential teacher of mathematics at West Point. Grant had encouragement from his instructor, and he kept up with his studies until transferred into the Southwest as part of the moves that were a prelude to the Mexican War.

His letters from the Mexican War period indicated he was very much in love. He was a young man uncertain about the future because he had been forced into the army by his father who thought he would save money by getting an education for his son at government expense. Grant had no desire to remain in the army any longer than his obligation. When he met the venerable Von Bismarck late in life, the Field Marshal wanted to hear all about Grant's military career and trade "war stories." Bismarck was amazed when the greatest soldier of the age told him that he entered the army with reluctance and left it with pleasure.

There is just no evidence that gives a clue about Grant's

relationship with his mother. The only revealing statement we have comes from his father. He said that Grant's characteristics came from his mother: his reticence, his shyness, his determination. Jesse Grant had enough self-knowledge to know that he, himself, was volatile, and pushy unlike his son. Jesse was not even an honest wheeler-dealer. One of his neighbors said he was the sort of man who would follow a dollar to hell — which is, perhaps, the sort of thing people said about one another in rural Ohio at that time.

We have to assume that Hannah Grant was just the opposite of Jesse and all we can really document is her devotion to the Methodist Church. We have to draw our own conclusions to the fact that she did not attend the inauguration of her son as president nor ever visit him in the White House.

There seems to have been ill feelings between the Grants and the Dents. The Dents inhabited the White House when Ulysses was president. "Colonel" Dent would sit in the lobby entertaining visitors with political commentary. Grant took this with a sense of humor. It was so outrageous. This old duffer saying that the whole country had gone to hell since the Democrats lost power when his own son-in-law was sitting upstairs as the President of the United States. It was past the point of embarrassment: It was so eccentric that it had its own special charm.

Grant may have known more financial hardship than any other man who ever achieved the office of president. Andrew Jackson was born poor and Grant was not. Grant achieved poverty and that is a completely different kettle of fish. Jackson was probably even better off than Andrew Johnson, but Johnson embarked on a career that started at the tailor shop and lead steadily onward and upward. On the other hand here is Grant, who as a young man achieved a piece of success in the army, a respectable rank commensurate with that of his classmates. There was nothing disgraceful about being an army captain. We live in such an age of inflation that when somebody is not a general, you think he is retarded. In those days promotion was almost impossible because officers remained in the army for the whole of their natural lives and unless there was a great military disaster these officers did not do much strenuous work and would live forever. This kept younger men in the lower ranks.

So Grant had not really done that badly — nothing disgraceful about being a captain at his age in 1854. For a man of that age, who was already established in a sense of having a family to provide for and having one of the best college educations available in the United States, to sink to such financial depths as Grant did in the late 1850s is something that must have had a searing effect. There is nothing disgraceful in being born poor, but there is something very damaging about having achieved poverty after receiving an education and whatever advantages the world had to offer. To be approaching the age of 40 and see one's self sinking in the world instead of rising had an effect on Grant that led him to think that people who were financially successful had more ability than they truly possessed.

As a military man he must have known how to judge officers better than he knew how to judge civilians. Every once in a while Grant, who had a talent for making bad appointments, came up with inspired ones. It should not be forgotten that in his own Grant-like way he conceived the idea of appointing Colonel Parker, an Indian, as

Commissioner of Indian Affairs. Hamilton Fish was an excellent choice for Secretary of State.

In Grant's administration he had to draw on the pool of the Republican talent available then. This was a great handicap. It was not a good age; it was not a good time for men in politics.

Captain Grant was not an alcoholic. If he were an alcoholic he would have a problem in drinking any time, even in a moderate way. And there is plenty of evidence that Grant did drink — moderately, for the rest of his life. Furthermore, as somebody who had that reputation, everybody kept their eye on Grant. It was impossible for him to take a drink without somebody watching out of the corner of his eye to notice that he did not have another drink. Everytime he turned over his wine glass, as a signal for declining wine, somebody seems to have taken note of it. It was almost a no-win situation.

He may have been a person who did not hold liquor well in part because he was a rather small man. There are people who can drink a lot without showing the effects. There must be a relationship between alcohol and body weight. Until Grant reached the White House he was probably underweight, and more likely to be affected by what he does drink than others. He was one of the few people who gained weight while he was president, but few noticed that. Certainly by the time his second administration came to an end, he had gained substantial weight. He had never been in a position where he had so little to do. It is difficult today to conceive the slight burden of the presidency, particularly in view of the excessive rhetoric to which we are exposed about the awesome burden of that fearful responsibility.

Grant must have gone on a few happy sprees as a

young man. This kind of drinking certainly would not lead to aggresive behavior. It was probably a reflection either of the tension under which he lived at the moment, which would be the case during the Civil War, or of his depression on the Pacific Coast at the prospect of being separated from his family for an indefinite period of time. The root of that drinking was the poverty; he had to put up with inflated Pacific Coast prices, an inadequate officer's salary, and, when he tried to make money it ended costing him instead. And having come from a relatively well-to-do family and having married into an even more well-to-do family, this sort of thing weighed heavily on Brevet Captain Grant. The army was definitely a dead end. Almost every West Point educated officer who achieved great military reputation during the Civil War resigned from the army prior to the Civil War.

In 1852 Sam Grant had a strong looking face, a square chin with a cleft, with eyes large and wide apart. He made you feel like he was interested in you and was concerned. He wore his chestnut brown hair in a modish look, below the ears on the sides. He weighed about 135 pounds, was under five feet eight inches tall, but no weakling. One English lady saw him as an honest and blunt soldier with a great talent for silence.

And strange for his country upbringing, he did not like to hunt. Grant could not stand the sight of red meat, or blood: "well-done" was his beef style. Grant did fish on occasion, but was bored easily with it. His first choice of recreation was to ride a good horse through the countryside.

Grant had no shrewd, merchant-like qualities about him: smart enough, ambitious for profit, but really unable to clinch deals or price properly, or invest sagaciously, or take an advantage. No doubt he was too trusting in his dealing with others. This became a serious problem when he was elected as the youngest man to become president to that time.

This then was Brevet Captain Grant in the summer of 1852. He was a respected, but average professional officer with a good war record. He had made an excellent marriage and was deeply in love. A solid fellow, a good friend, and a proven soldier in a fight. He was the last person his contemporaries would have picked for greatness.

Now let us turn to a more specific account of U. S. Grant during his West Coast years. The 4th Infantry received orders in the late spring of 1852 to move to New York City in preparation for its assignment to the Pacific Division headquarters in far-off California. Grant sent his pregnant wife and son to his father's home in Bethel, Ohio, near Cincinnati, while he tackled his quartermaster business of moving troops and equipment out of Sackets Harbor, New York.

By June 17, 1852, the 4th Infantry had assembled at Fort Columbus, Governors Island, New York. That small chunk of land lay about one mile off the tip of Manhattan connected to the Battery by a shuttle of rowboats, barges and an occasional steam ferry. Fort Columbus, with single story, long stone structures and forty foot high walls, was completed in 1833 to protect the entrance to the East River and New York Harbor.

Except for a few wives who were billeted in rooms not needed by the artillery company stationed there, most of the regiment went under canvas. The tents were stifling in unseasonable hot weather and sparsely furnished with trunks for chairs and bunks for beds.

The regimental quartermaster was busy getting ready to sail, "All preparation for starting devolvs [sic] on me," he wrote Julia. And the more Grant thought about it, the more he was certain that Julia could not accompany him. "I think on the whole it is a dangerous experiment for the ladies to go to Calafornia [sic]. . . Some of the ladies of the 2nd Infantry who went with their husbands in 1848 have returned and do not intend going back . . ."[11]

Brevet Captain Grant was concerned about what lay ahead for the seven hundred persons who were scheduled for the move and was anxious to be off. "The later in the season we put off going the worse it will be crossing the Isthmus," he wrote.[12] Also, Ulysses was worried about his and Julia's good friend John Gore. "I think it very foolish in the Major going. His health is such that he can get a sick leave by asking in a minuet [sic]."[13]

---

[11]Grant, *Papers*, p. 238. No attempt has been made in these pages to correct Grant's interestingly inaccurate, and often resourceful spelling.

[12]*Ibid.*

[13]*Ibid.*, p. 241.

Chapter II

"We Sail Directly For The Isthmus"

At 2:00 p.m., on July 5, 1852, eight companies of the 4th Infantry with the band and headquarters departed from Governors Island, New York, for the Isthmus of Panama on the steamship *Ohio*.[1] The oaken, side-wheeler was built in New York to carry 330 passengers on three decks in comfort. Her flying-serpent's figurehead and extended bowsprit, gave the *Ohio* a sprightly look.[2]

The *Ohio* had been on the New York-Panama run since the fall of 1849. For an earlier voyage, the *New York Commercial Advertiser* had reported that "the steam ship *Ohio* leaves this afternoon at 3 o'clock for Navy Bay, with five hundred and fifty passengers for California." *The Shipping and Commercial List*, and *New-York Price Current* also advertised the sailing: "The splendid double engine steam ship *OHIO* (3000 tons burthen,) J. F. Schenck,

---

[1] The title of this chapter is the opening sentence of a July 5, 1852 letter from Grant to his wife on the day he sailed for the Pacific Coast. Grant, *Papers*, p. 247.

[2] John Haskell Kemble, *The Panama Route* (Berkeley, 1943), p. 239. Dr. Kemble is recognized nationally as a foremost maritime scholar and the leading historian of the Isthmus crossing period.

U.S.N., Commander, will sail... direct for *CHAGRES*, connecting... for San Francisco on arrival of the passengers and mail at Panama."[3] The passengers on this trip of the *Ohio* were the last ever landed at Chagres by the big steamers; after November, 1851, steamship lines disembarked their passengers at Aspinwall.

During the voyage, Lieutenant Commander J. Finley Schenck captained the *Ohio*, and fifty-six-year-old Lieutenant Colonel Benjamin Louis Eulalie de Bonneville led the military. The 4th Infantry had been commanded by Colonel William Whistler of Maryland, an army regular now too ancient for field service, who was placed on an indefinite leave of absence.[4]

The trip was uncomfortable from the start. The ship was terribly crowded since the 651 military men, and over 50 of their family members, were pushed onto the steamer already loaded with men on their way to the goldfields of California. Grant counted more than 1,100 on board. Moreover, they sailed amid upsetting reports to the senior medical officer, Major Charles Stuart Tripler, that a cholera epidemic was in full swing on the Isthmus. Tripler's wife, Eunice, who thought Bonneville "a very stupid man mentally," did not accompany her husband to California but she recorded his distress:

> Dr. Tripler thought it a great cruelty to start them at a season when cholera was raging on the Isthmus... Before leaving New York, [he] wrote the Surgeon General it was murder to

---

[3]Newspapers cited in Georgia Willis Read, "The Chagres River Route to California in 1851" *Qtly. of the Calif. Hist. Soc.* (Mar. 1929), p. 7.

[4]Col. William Whistler nominally commanded the 4th Infantry from July, 1845, until he retired Oct., 1861. Grant served under him at Detroit and Sackets Harbor, New York, 1849-1852. The Grants knew Colonel and Mrs. Whistler, and their daughter, Louise, rather well.

attempt the crossing of the Isthmus then. But the reply was it would be 'quickly over.'[5]

Fortunately, the climate was delightful during the voyage from New York to Aspinwall. Grant wrote that "We have been blessed with remarkable fine weather from the beginning."[6] Every evening the military band played for dancing. The passengers got acquainted by cardplaying, fishing, spotting whales, and easy conversation about what lay ahead. But with little room for exercise in cramped quarters and the temperature rising each day, inactivity and boredom took their toll. Sometimes, according to Grant, the cabins were "so insufferably hot that no one can stay there."[7] And the young captain, who later traveled the world's sealanes with hardly a stomach quiver, was among those who became seasick.

Sam Grant was popular among his fellow officers. Those who had served with him in Mexico especially respected him and held him in high esteem. Second Lieutenant Henry C. Hodges met Grant for the first time just before sailing. Hodges described him as "a thin, quiet, reticent man, full of kindly and generous feeling for those about him."[8]

Although Grant had the reputation of being a professional and giving close and strict attention to his duties,[9] Bonneville, at first, wanted another quartermaster. Per-

[5]Louis A. Arthur, ed., *Eunice Tripler; Some Notes of Her Personal Recollections* (New York, 1910), pp. 106-08.
[6]Grant, *Papers*, p. 248.
[7]*Ibid.*
[8]Henry C. Hodges to William Conant Church, Jan. 7, 1897; William C. Church Papers, Manuscript Div., Library of Cong. Cited hereafter as Hodges (Church Papers).   [9]*Ibid.*

haps this was because Grant was thought to be Whistler's man or for some other unknown reason. There was opposition on the part of other 4th Infantry officers to making a change, however, and, since Bonneville was an indecisive commander, the matter was dropped. The fact was that Captain Grant preferred Whistler as his commanding officer rather than Bonneville. Even after arriving on the West Coast, Grant wrote to Julia: "We are somewhat in hope that Col. Whistler will join us here. He writes that he is determined to come..."[10]

Years later, the *Ohio's* master would recall Sam Grant and the trip to Panama. Schenck thought Grant a very quiet person who took the world as he found it, but who could be counted upon to have opinions and defend them. The *Ohio's* captain did not like Bonneville, thought him hasty and unsure in his actions, always being bailed out by his sensible quartermaster. As the ship steamed southward the navy captain and the sleepless, young army captain would walk up and down the deck at night talking of many things and becoming better acquainted. Schenck found Grant an educated, intelligent man, and one whose mind took hold of ideas, grasped them strongly and digested them thoroughly.[11]

Another passenger aboard the *Ohio* remembered the day when some of the officers were having a difference of opinion on the main deck, while Grant sat by himself on the opposite side, out of hearing. As the argument got warmer, and the prospect of agreement less, the regimental adjutant suggested: "I tell you, fellows, how we

---

[10]Grant, *Papers*, p. 287.

[11]Hamlin Garland, "Grant's Quiet Years at Northern Posts," *McClure's Magazine*, Mar. 1, 1897, pp. 406-07. Garland footnotes that the Schenck quotation is from an interview first published in the *New York Herald*.

will settle this. Let's go across the deck and refer the whole matter to long-headed Sam, and whatever may be his decision we will abide by it." This was not the only dispute during that boring trip that "long-headed Sam" was called upon to mediate.[12]

One source of amusement which helped pass the time was the group's careful observation of the new commander who was definitely a "character." Bonneville, old for a frontiersman, was a small man, deliberate and very much the dandy. He carried a cane and wore a large, white, stiff beaver hat to cover his bald dome. His sense of dignity and his hat never deserted him all the miles from New York Harbor to the shore of the broad Columbia.

Certain junior members of the 4th, allied with well-hidden sailors, would shout with great irreverence, "Where did you get that hat?" as Bonneville stomped around the deck each day. Try as he might the old warrior could not catch a single one of those pesky jokers, adding to the general merriment of the bored passengers. One observer thought Bonneville "a most gallant and experienced officer, [but with] a somewhat arbitrary and testy temper."[13] Anticipation was high, however, and a crusty commanding officer was not that unusual.

Bonneville was born in Paris in 1796 and graduated from West Point in 1815. In the early 1830s, on leave from the army, he led a three-year trapping expedition through the Rocky Mountains that brought him considerable publicity. It was the first major exploration since that of Lewis and Clark, and it took Bonneville down the

---

[12] William C. Church, *Ulysses S. Grant* (New York, 1897), p. 50.

[13] William S. Lewis, ed., *Reminiscences of Delia B. Sheffield* (Seattle, 1924), p. 5 (cited hereafter as Lewis, *Sheffield*). The author has in his private library Mr. Lewis' autographed copy which he gave to the 4th Infantry in 1924.

Columbia River into Hudson's Bay territory. He never reached one of his objectives, Fort Vancouver, but won a reputation with a great assist from the well-known author, Washington Irving, who upon Bonneville's return, edited and published the trip's journal as the *Adventures of Captain Bonneville, U.S.A.*

Although criticized for some commercial aspects of his exploration, he was recognized as a frontier leader.

As the ship plowed on, Grant already had experienced the lonely forces that later engulfed him. Trying to see the bright side, he noted to Julia that his expectations were high for "this move. I expect by it to do something for myself."[14] But, loner that he was, Grant spent his hours walking back and forth, head down and deep in thought. One young passenger noted during every day and every evening he spent his time "pacing the deck and smoking, silent and solitary." She noticed also that he smoked too much. Fellow passengers considered Sam Grant a thoughtful and serious officer, not given to light talk, but "affable in manner." When old Bonneville became arbitrary and difficult, it was the quartermaster who helped to smooth over the unpleasantness.[15]

The inactivity of the voyage ended on July 16th when the *Ohio* reached Aspinwall (later named Colón) in Limon Bay, starting point for the Isthmus crossing. The town, named after the Pacific Mail Steamship Company's first president and a founder of the Panama Railroad Company, was built on a marshy island from earth and rock brought back from the railroad construction site.[16]

---

[14]Grant, *Papers*, p. 249.   [15]Lewis, *Sheffield*, pp. 5-6.

[16]Kemble, *op. cit.*, p. 23. In May, 1861, President Lincoln apparently discussed with his cabinet the appointment of Aspinwall as Quartermaster General. See *Quartermaster General of the Union Army: a Biography of M. C. Meigs* (New York, 1959), p. 161.

Lt. Col. Benjamin Louis Eulalie de Bonneville.
Courtesy, Wyoming State Arch., Museums & Hist. Dept.

The fill was dumped in a swamp which had been described as stinking and unbearable with a generous population of sandflies, mosquitoes, snakes and venomous insects.

During the rainy season Aspinwall was a mess. The unpaved streets were deep in water with makeshift, raised planks providing "sidewalks." Grant wondered how anybody could live there and why anybody would want to. But the town flourished with a mixture of American and Spanish culture; it even had its own English-language newspaper. Aspinwall was the Atlantic terminus for the "Panama Route" which became the premier link between the United States' two coastal areas. The overland passage, with its well-known difficulties, and the long trip "round the horn" could not compete with the Panama Route for speed or dependability. Between 1848 and 1869 thousands of travelers and tons of merchandise jostled between Chagres or Aspinwall, on the Atlantic, and Panama City on the Pacific. A loose but organized network of small paddle-wheelers, native canoes, mule trains, and finally, the railroad, became an integral part of America's transportation system. Until the golden spike riveted the nation together in 1869, people and messages could not travel between the Atlantic and Pacific Coasts more swiftly or surely than by way of Panama.[17]

When it was first discovered in 1501 the Isthmus was called Darien, which for years was used synonymously with Panama. Just a few degrees north of the equator, the Isthmus is so narrow that you can see both oceans from several low peaks. Only one mountain in the vicinity of the crossing has an elevation over 3,000 feet; most are under 650 feet. The geography is a bit confusing. The

---

[17]Kemble, *op. cit.*, p. vi, and author's interviews with Dr. Kemble.

Isthmus is east of Florida, and lies generally east and west: thus, to reach the Pacific from the Atlantic the traveler went south.

Many rivers rise in the mountains, but only one is identified forever with the affairs of that region. Christopher Columbus named it Rio Lagartos, River of Alligators; Balboa called it the Chagres. Henry Morgan the pirate was there, as was Francis Drake and a host of conquistadors and adventurers. Originally it was the Spanish river gateway to the wealth of the Incas and one author believed that the Chagres was the world's most valuable river.[18]

The Chagres, which today is mostly submerged by Canal Zone lakes, was about 120 miles long and several hundred feet wide. Depending on the season, the river could be five feet deep for miles, with some places twenty-five feet in depth. During the frequent flash floods the river could rise forty feet in a single day. The Chagres usually flowed steadily, curving in and out, with some shoals and rapids, bordered by heavily-jungled banks all the way from Cruces down to the Caribbean. The river was the dominant physical and historical feature of the Isthmus, and the California-bound travelers were impressed.

Panama's climate is even, month in and month out. Early morning temperatures are a pleasant 72-74 degrees; by midday, they are up to 84-90 degrees. The wet "winter season" is from June to November and the dry season is usually January to April (December and May are considered intermediary months). It rains every month of the year; annual rainfall is as high as twelve *feet* on the Atlantic side and half of that on the Pacific.

---

[18]John Easter Minter, *The Chagres* (New York, 1948), p. 5.

The Panama Railroad, the marvel of its day, was pushed through the jungles and over the rivers by thousands of workers and, after a struggle of almost five years, completed in February, 1855. One historian looked upon the construction of the Panama Railroad as being as great, if not greater, an undertaking as the building of the canal. It was the first transcontinental railroad in the world.[19]

But in mid-1852 when the 4th Infantry disembarked, the railroad had been completed only to Barbacoas almost twenty miles inland (five miles short of Gorgona) where a four-hundred-foot bridge over the Chagres was being constructed.[20] The first time California-bound passengers were carried over the railroad was seven months before the 4th Infantry arrived when 700 passengers from the *Georgia* took the rails about eight miles up the line over the objections of the local railroad management. They feared it would inhibit the progress of the work.[21]

Upon arrival in Aspinwall, it became apparent that the 4th Infantry faced serious trouble. The Pacific Mail Steamship Company agents who had contracted to move the regiment from the Atlantic to the Pacific were not prepared for their arrival. In-transit gold seekers had bought or rented all the accommodations, inflated the price of labor and mules, and created havoc with the transport system.

To ease the problem the agent suggested that the regiment split into small parties and take two routes. At this time the normal path to the Pacific was in three stages:

[19]C.L.G. Anderson, *Old Panama* (New York, 1938), p. 10.
[20]David Howarth, *Panama* (New York, 1966), p. 185, and interview with Dr. Kemble, Aug. 1978.
[21]Read, *op. cit.*, p. 10.

the unfinished Panama Railroad to the Chagres River at Barbacoas; native boats upriver to the head of navigation (Gorgona or Cruces, depending on the season); and a mule train on into Panama City. The troops, who had expected to ride after going upriver as far as possible, were now ordered to march to Panama after reaching Gorgona.

Gorgona and Cruces were settled because they were the best spots at the head of navigation on the Chagres. Each place had several respectable forwarding houses and hotels, owned by Americans.[22] Miller's Hotel, the French Hotel, and the Spanish and American House were in Gorgona. In Cruces, the leading hostelry was Ran Runnels' American Hotel, which featured, in late 1851, supper, cot, and breakfast for two dollars. The village houses of the natives were usually huts, made of canes and dried palm tree leaves.[23] The population moved up and down with the level of the river since the commission merchants, transportation agents, and hotel-keepers switched from Gorgona to Cruces for the rainy season. Also, as many as five hundred Americans awaiting ships to San Francisco would lie over in the villages in a vain attempt to escape Panama City's high cost of living.

Led by Grant, the band, civilians, all regimental baggage, and those who were ill, were to take the Cruces route where a few pack mules would be available. Col. Bonneville would take the main body upriver to Gor-

---

[22]Chauncey D. Griswold, *The Isthmus of Panama* (New York, 1852), p. 46.

[23]E. L. Autenrieth. *Isthmus of Panama* (New York, 1851), pp. 9, 14; Read, *op. cit.*, p. 13. Ran Runnels, a busy entrepreneur, was one of the leading American residents of Panama. Not only did he own the French Hotel in Gorgona and the American Hotel in Cruces, but he contracted for road improvements on the Cruces Trail and was the founder of Runnels Isthmus Guard, an important railroad security service. *Panama Star*, June 25, 1852; Kemble, *op. cit.*, pp. 173-76.

gona then overland to the Pacific coast. The two groups were then to meet where the routes united, about five miles above Panama.

Grant's group at the start included: Dr. Tripler; Brevet Major and Mrs. John H. Gore, old and dear friends from Detroit and Sackets Harbor, New York, with their little son; Brevet Captain Henry Davis Wallen, 2nd, commanding the escort company, his wife Anne, sons Harry and Eddy and daughter Nann; Second Lieutenant John Withers, commanding the guard; the wives of Second Lieutenants Slaughter, Collins and Underwood; Eljah E. Camp and Mr. Alford; Sergeant D. G. Sheffield and his sixteen-year-old bride, Delia; Drum Major Elderkin and his young wife, Mary; Mr. and Mrs. Lynch with three children; wives of enlisted men, including Mrs. Kelley and Margaret Getz, who had been Julia Grant's household helper; and a small contingent of Catholic Sisters of Charity, who joined the group on the trail.

Sgt. James Elderkin, the drum major, told how the journey started: "We had Grant's superintendence in packing all the arms putting forty in each sack, and then the sailors sewed them up. We had to pack them on mules across the isthmus . . . Grant staid until the stores were all started . . . [and] had to look after the health of his soldiers and the people going with him . . ."[24]

Most of the regiment, seven companies and the regimental headquarters, moved promptly by rail to the river crossing, and then by native "bungo" dugouts to the town of Gorgona. The trail from Gorgona to Panama City, with all its shortcomings, was not more than twenty miles in length, crossing the Continental Divide

---

[24]Hamlin Garland Papers, Dept. of Special Coll., Univ. of So. Cal. Library, Los Angeles (cited hereafter as Garland Papers). Interview with Drum Major Elderkin (cited hereafter as "Garland-Elderkin Interview").

by an easier route than the Cruces trail. In normal weather, only the first five miles or so were really bad; the rest, with certain exceptions was unremarkable. The route, however, was good only during the dry season because it ran so close to rivers, streams, and marshland. When it rained, the clay and marshes were turned into impassable mud with as many as nineteen stream crossings. At the trail's "Half-way House," two large tents had been set up to provide some protection and a rest area for traveling Americans. In July, 1852, the Gorgona trail was a morass, and the troops were unable to carry their normal equipment. Bonneville, leading the main body, slogged to the Pacific in two or three days and boarded the waiting steamship.

Grant, as regimental quartermaster, was dispatched further upriver to Cruces with one company for escort carrying camp and garrison equipment, tents, mess chests, kettles, and supervising soldiers, their wives and children, and miscellaneous civilians. This necessitated a harrowing trip long remembered.

Grant's bungo boat journey with this diverse company was not without incident and thoroughly unpleasant. He later recalled that the "boats carried thirty to forty passengers each. The crews consisted of six men to a boat, armed with long poles... [and] not inconveniently burdened with clothing." Top speed as they poled along "was a mile to a mile and a half an hour... against the current of the river."[25]

Delia Sheffield never forgot the trip up the Chagres in those boats. Years later she wrote of the strong and swift current which made progress so slow. When night came

---

[25]*Personal Memoirs of U. S. Grant* (New York, 1885), p. 195 (cited hereafter as Grant, *Memoirs*).

the boats were tied to the bank while the natives "went up to a little village [where] they caroused all night . . . while we sat in shivering terror in the boats, kept awake by their shouting and fearing an attack from the drunken barbarians." When at last the long night was over, the journey was resumed only to see knife fights break out among the boat crews which greatly frightened the women and children of the party. Delia praised Captain Grant who "in his quiet unassuming manner seemed to provide for everyone and we all had the highest praise for him."[26]

Wallen recalled that while he and Grant were moving up the Chagres a report came back that a boat had capsized and those on board had been drowned. But the report proved false, and after they determined that all the army wives were safe, the trip upriver continued.[27]

Grant got his party safely to Cruces, which was five miles or so above Gorgona, but found Edmund Duckworth, the contractor, could produce neither animals nor native porters. "There was not a mule . . . in the place," Grant noted.[28] The town was a lively spot, crowded with natives and travelers moving down the streets at all hours. The noise made sleep almost impossible. Cruces had a church and Gorgona had "a place they call by that name, though to me it looked like anything but a church," observed one American.[29] Both villages had taverns, ample whiskey, and more than a few whores.

It was a trying time at Cruces that summer of 1852 with terrible weather, the cholera, and inadequate shelter.

[26]Lewis, *Sheffield*, pp. 6-7.
[27]Frank A. Burr, *Life of General Grant* (Philadelphia, 1885), p. 113.
[28]Grant, *Memoirs*, p. 196.
[29]*Journal of Henry Sturdivant from December 8, 1849, of Cumberland, Maine*, Henry E. Huntington Library, San Marino, California, p. 7.

The Chagres River near Gorgona.

The Old Las Cruces-Panama Trail, 1914.
Both photographs reprinted with permission of
The Society of American Military Engineers.

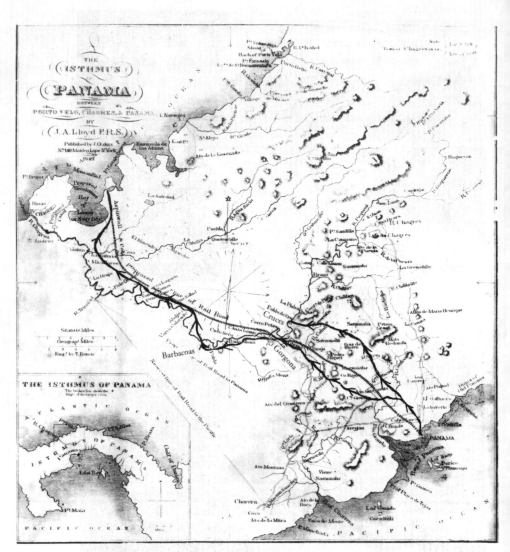

The Isthmus of Panama.
Map by J.A. Lloyd and published by J. Oakes,
New York City in 1849. The map has been modified to
highlight the crossing of the U.S. Army's 4th Infantry
Regiment in July 1852 (black line with arrows).
Courtesy, Huntington Library, San Marino, California.

The situation worsened as the baggage was exposed to heavy rains and became soggy, making large amounts of it unuseable. Several of the party guarding the equipment died of the cholera. To minimize the risk and make progress, Captain Sam sent the escort company on to Panama City and stayed behind to organize those left. Now with Grant, to look after the women and the sick, were Lieutenant Withers' shrinking guard force and Dr. Tripler. Grant remained until everyone started "on mules or in litters... excepting one or two who were so low with the cholera that they could not be carried. These persons were removed to comfortable quarters, the services of a Doctor employed, and arrangements made for their transmission through to Panama as soon as they should recover sufficiently."[30] Grant recalled that "I was left alone with the sick and the soldiers who had families."[31] Drum Major Elderkin later reminisced:

> [Grant] was afraid [my wife and I] would take the cholera; he took great interest in us, and told me that I had better start and go to Panama, and he gave me twenty dollars and said... If you cannot get a mule, you had better start off alone. Your wife cannot go with skirts on. So I put onto my wife a pair of my white pantaloons, and a white shirt... I told Captain Grant that I had everything but a coat, and he said, I have one that will just fit her, and he went to his trunk and took out one, and then she put on my sword belt. He said, you buy some claret wine, and don't drink any water while you are on the way... When we got near Panama we met the American Counsel coming out on a horse, and he said, the cholera is in Panama...[32]

---

[30]Grant, *Papers*, pp. 270-71.   [31]Grant, *Memoirs*, p. 197.

[32]Garland-Elderkin Interview. There are several versions of the Elderkin interview in Garland's Papers. The author has used Garland's notes made after he talked with the old drum major in Detroit in 1896. In his handwriting, Garland describes Elderkin as "a hale and hearty old soldier, tall and straight and buoyant of bearing." Garland's subsequent publication of the interview corrects spelling and language, but the story remains essentially the same.

After waiting impatiently for three days, Grant set out to hire men and mules on his own and to move the remaining Americans to Panama City. He was exhibiting already the characteristics noted later by a grateful wartime president when he said of Grant, "Wherever he is, things move!" On July 21, 1852, army records show that Captain Sam contracted with José Ma. Saravia for the animals "at more than double the original price."[33]

Captain Wallen recalled that: "Grant in his capacity as quartermaster immediately perfected arrangements for sending [the ladies] across the Isthmus. This had to be done on hammocks thrown on the shoulders of [native] men with relays provided at convenient distances along the two days' journey" from Cruces to Panama City.[34]

Years later, Hodges wrote that:

> The most laborious part [of the entire trip] fell to the lot of our quartermaster, Captain Grant [whose] services were of the greatest importance and were highly creditable to himself and the regiment. His kindness and thoughtfulness were not confined to his own command, but he assisted many [civilian] passengers in getting across the Isthmus.[35]

The mule trip from Cruces to the Pacific Coast was usually two days, but Grant's party thought it would go on forever. It was even worse than the canoe journey. Only about twenty miles or so long, the "all weather road" from the north end of Cruces to Panama City was not worthy of the name. Rough, narrow, and hazardous, it was pocked with holes and coated with mud, but had a foundation of cobblestones. The Cruces route followed generally the ancient Spanish Trail connecting Panama with Porto Bello. A more northerly route which avoided

---

[33]Grant *Memoirs*, p. 198 and Grant's *Papers*, pp. 249-50.
[34]Burr, *op. cit.*, p. 113.   [35]Hodges (Church Papers).

marshlands, it had actually been "paved" centuries before and there was enough stonework remaining to give the mules some measure of footing. A modern writer noted that although this mule trip was over historic ground, few knew it and nobody cared.[36] A traveler of 1851 thought the Cruces trail was "a gutter of mud between rocks on a shelf at the top of a precipice."[37]

This more northerly Cruces trail avoided most of the streams, but it was more rugged than the Gorgona road, crossing a number of hilly spurs and zigzagging through ravines. One military traveler said traversing these spurs was like "a succession of stairs, up and down, with a hole in each step about three inches deep worn by the feet of the animals... into which your horse or mule inserts his foot, and you cannot make him place it anywhere else."[38] A knowledgeable Panama resident called it "certainly the worst and most fatiguing road we ever traveled."[39]

There were no high mountains in this sector but a large number of gullies which were loosely connected to form the highway. With the passage of years and thousands of hoofs, the gullies became deeper and deeper, always narrowing at the bottom. Most were so tight that one-way traffic was a necessity. Although the natives whooped and hollered when entering a gully, two parties would inevitably meet in the middle, and arguments about who had to back up were loud, long, and sometimes violent.

The scenery was exotic, with tropical beauty all

[36] Howarth, *op. cit.*, p. 174.

[37] Oscar Lewis, *Sea Routes to the Gold Fields* (New York, 1949), p. 182. Lewis writes that Henry Sturdivant was this traveler, but the author's study of Sturdivant's journal does not confirm this.

[38] Roland Dennis Hussey, *Spanish Colonial Trails in Panama* (Mexico, 1939), p. 60.

[39] Autenrieth, *op. cit.*, p. 12.

around. A tangled jungle of green, coconut trees, tropical ferns, and vivid orange and scarlet flowers were there for the travelers to view. Monkeys chattered, parrots kept up in incessant screeching, wild turkeys sat in the treetops, pheasants and pigeons flew in large numbers, but in single-file, plodding along the muddy mule track, Grant's group had no eye for the splendor of the scene. The ladies rode or walked or were carried in hammocks; there was little agreement as to which method of torture was the worst. A few of the women who walked fainted from the heat and ended up with raw and bleeding feet. Grant recorded that Anne Wallen arrived in Panama weighing only eighty-four pounds, a substantial loss.

Attractive, clear springs were seen beside the trail at decent intervals, but Captain Grant "warned [the party] against drinking any of the water . . . as he said it would cause fever."[40] Speed was limited by three factors: the animal's inclination, the traveler's seat, and the trail itself, which was almost without bottom. Along with pots, kettles, and other equipment, Grant had to transport the mountain of knapsacks the main party could not carry over the foot trail from Gorgona to Panama.

As members of Grant's group became ill they would slide off the backs of the mules, but indifferent natives would toss them back up to continue the jolting ride. The mules, small but sturdy, were bearing loads out of all proportion to their size, so they too became weary as the trip went on. One of the Catholic Sisters contacted the cholera at Cruces, but Grant was able to keep her in a hammock all the way to Panama.

Captain Sam watched Henry Wallen's children struggling to keep up and never doubted that his decision to

---

[40] Lewis, *Sheffield*, p. 8.

leave pregnant Julia and his infant son, Fred, behind, was the right one. Every child Fred's age or younger, and there were twenty of them, either died on the crossing or shortly thereafter.[41] "My dearest," he wrote, "you never could have crossed the Isthmus at this season . . ."[42] Grant did not know that Ulysses S. Grant, Jr., had been born as he prepared to move down the Cruces trail.

Near exhaustion, half-dead with fatigue, tired and unkempt from exposure to heat and rain, the travelers continued on. The women and children who made this hard and weary trip remembered, all their lives, the kindness and self-sacrifice of the officers who helped them walk across the Isthmus in 1852. And Ulysses S. Grant was remembered most.[43]

The explorer Lionel Gisborne, going in the opposite direction, passed Captain Sam's party on the Cruces trail. He noted that there were not enough mules for the army wives and that: "Modesty gave way to necessity; some had most wisely put on trowsers, and discarded the petticoat, but most of them tucked this feminine garment to about the knee and tramped along through mud and over rocks with greater spirit than the men."[44]

Just before reaching Panama City the Cruces and Gorgona routes joined at Cruz de Cardenas where there were several houses and one last river to cross. But now the trail flattened out, several smaller avenues from both north and south joined in, and the road became a highway. Farms were seen on both sides; carts hauling produce, water-carriers, and miscellaneous travelers all joined the pack mule parade. Saddle-sore, tired and dirty, the swaying, three-day ride came to an end and Grant's

[41]Grant, *Papers*, p. 288.   [42]*Ibid.*, p. 252.
[43]Lewis, *Sheffield*, pp. 9-10.   [44]Howarth, *op. cit.*, p. 182.

straggling, wet party first viewed the Pacific Ocean on July 25 or 26. Grant summed up: "The horrors of the road, in the rainy season, are beyond description."[45]

Now closed up, the 4th Infantry found Panama filled with frustrated and impatient men, brothels, saloons and gambling dens. Temporary camps had grown up on the outskirts of town and it was here that malaria, yellow fever, dysentery, and the deadliest disease, cholera, raged.

Panama in 1852 was a town of contrasts. Many of the structures were one-story, thatched roof, tumbledown adobes enclosed by low stone walls, but there were also great stone buildings, paved streets and a lively, established society. Gambling appeared to be the principal business done by the natives, observed one gold seeker as he passed through.[46] The American newspaper of the day reported that the summer of 1852 was an especially active one in Panama City with an estimated 10,000 natives, 350 permanent resident foreigners (mostly Americans), hundreds of California-bound passengers milling around, and building going on at a rapid pace. The center of business, and indeed the center of town, was the Plaza dominated by the ancient cathedral with its twin bell towers. Merchandise of every description was being handled under the tropic sun and between rain showers as it was off-loaded from ships. On July 28 Grant had no trouble buying 249 blankets to replace those lost or damaged by rains.[47]

---

[45]Grant, *Papers*, p. 252. It is clear that the final leg of the Isthmus crossing was considered the most difficult by the travelers of the period 1849-1855. The author's study of journals and other primary source materials shows a great similarity of accounts. As Howarth's *Panama* summarizes (p. 174) the travelers were not impressed with the strange sights and sounds of the jungle, but by the mud, the narrowness of the track and the mules jolting gait. This is what they remembered and what they wrote about.

[46]Henry Sturdivant's journal, p. 8.   [47]Grant, *Papers*, p. 251.

The streets were dirty, the natives (mestizos) were mostly disagreeable, and the few Spanish were not interested in the crowds of Americans. There was a goodly supply of cheap, fresh, and delicious fruit; restaurants advertised full variety menus.

The English-language newspaper, *Panama Star,* was published about once a week and chronicled the civic issues of the day: unfair and excessive taxes on foreigners, the new Panama Water Stock Company, "the second most important venture on the Isthmus," behind the railroad, of course, and the dismal record of the New Granada government on public works improvements.[48]

Meanwhile, Bonneville's party had reached Panama City on July 20 and was barged to the *Golden Gate* which was standing off Taboga to transport the troops to San Francisco. But disaster struck these troops resting from their wet march: on their second day aboard, the cholera broke out. Dr. Tripler had not arrived, so the soldiers enlisted civilian medical help.

Captain Wallen, sent ahead by Grant, later recalled that as he neared Panama word reached him that the epidemic had broken out there also. His company moved directly to the ship and "that night one of my men was taken with the cholera, and by daylight the next morning there were several cases on board."[49] Delia Sheffield described the scene in Panama Bay:

> Captain Grant, as quartermaster, and the surgeons did every-
> thing in their power to check the spread of the disease, and to
> alleviate the sufferings of the stricken ones. Too much praise
> cannot be given them for their tireless energy and great
> presence of mind during this outbreak of cholera. It was not an

[48] The description of Panama City in the summer of 1852 comes from the June 17, June 26, 1852 issues in the Honnold Library, Claremont, Calif.

[49] Burr, *op. cit.*, pp. 113-14.

easy task to control almost seven hundred men during a siege of cholera, for they grew nervous and panic-stricken and Captain Grant had not only the sick ones to contend with but also the well.[50]

The drum major's wife, Mrs. Elderkin, related that "Captain Grant had a tremendous responsibility... but he did the work with as much system as though he had been quartered at" an established army post. She saw Grant as a man of iron, seldom sleeping, who seemed to take a personal interest in each case. "He was like a ministering angel to us all."[51]

Captain Wallen told of an incident that touched Ulysses most personally:

Grant was one of the coolest men in all these trying emergencies I ever saw. I remember during that dismal time in Panama bay that he, a Major Gore and myself sat playing a friendly game of euchre, when Major Gore suddenly dropped his hand, turned pale and said: 'My God, I have got the Cholera!' Grant, in the most nonchalant way, undertook to quiet his fears by saying: 'No Major, you have only eaten something that does not agree with you.' But the doctor was summoned, and although everything possible was done, Gore died before morning, the only officer we lost.[52]

The *Panama Herald*, in a July 27, 1852, editorial, reported that the 4th Infantry had been pouring into Panama City and moving out to the *Golden Gate* throughout the week.

A portion of these troops came through in good time, and apparently in the enjoyment of health. A goodly number, however, sickened and died on the road... [The number of dead] must have been considerable... There is great fault

[50]Lewis, *Sheffield*, p. 10.   [51]Garland, "Grant's Quiet Years," p. 408.
[52]Burr, *op. cit.*, p. 114.

somewhere and just censure should be meted out . . . the whole business reflects great discredit upon the United States.[53]

Edward Flint, the steamship company agent, became concerned about the contamination of the *Golden Gate* and insisted on moving everybody to a hulk (the company called it a storeship) off Taboga in Panama Bay while the ship was fumigated. Later, that makeshift hospital became so crowded with sick that the troops and their families were moved to tents on smaller Flamenco Island.[54] Flamenco was the outer one of a group of small, rocky islands a few miles offshore from the city. Beginning in early 1853 it was utilized by the Pacific Mail as a major base when the company moved from Taboga. Eventually the new base had storehouses, carpenter and blacksmith shops, overhaul facilities, and a large inventory of coal. But in 1852 Flamenco was barren, with only a few houses and some farmland.

By August 3, the disease seemed to run its course, but the experienced Pacific Mail agent, fearing its reappearance, would dispatch the *Golden Gate* with only 450 passengers (the number of berths available). The rest of the 4th's group was left behind with one company to act as attendants, the Pacific Mail agreeing to supply these people with necessities of life and to bring them to California as quickly as possible.

The wooden "steam clipper" *Golden Gate* with her spread eagle figurehead, was a new and popular ship held in high regard by knowledgeable travelers and looked

[53]*Grant Association Newsletter* (January 1969), pp. 1-2.

[54]Grant, *Memoirs*, p. 199, incorrectly called this island, "Flamengo," several maps of the day did also. The correct name was, and is, Flamenco. *See* Dr. Kemble, *National Geographic,* and Anderson's *Old Panama* maps, among others.

like an uncrowded paradise to the 4th. New York-built in 1850-1851 at a cost of $483,000, she was the first sidewheel steamer designed for the Panama-California route after the true nature of the trade was known. The *Golden Gate*, at 2,067 tons and 269 feet long, was considered large, swift and comfortable.[55]

After spending three weeks on the Isthmus, on August 5, Bonneville's regiment, having lost almost one hundred soldiers to the cholera, departed for California. About 35,000 travelers made an Isthmus crossing that year but none suffered more than the 4th Infantry. The crossing was over, but a lifelong impression had been made upon the young captain.[56]

Hodges recalled that General Grant in his late years talked more about his experience on the Isthmus than any of his great campaigns during the War of the Rebellion.[57] The crossing left Grant with the permanent dream of a canal in which travelers would not have to set foot on those jungle shores.[58]

---

[55]Information on the *Golden Gate* from the following sources: Kemble, *op. cit.*, p. 228; Oscar Lewis, *op. cit.*, p. 260; Robert W. Parkinson's selection in *Gold Rush Steamers* (San Francisco, 1958) and David I. Folkman, Jr., *The Nicaragua Route* (Salt Lake City, 1972) p. 34.

[56]Lloyd Lewis, *Letters from Lloyd Lewis* (Boston, 1950) p. 78.

[57]Hodges (Church Papers).

[58]Lloyd Lewis, *op. cit.*, pp. 77-78. In his first presidential message to Congress, Grant recommended an American canal connecting the two oceans. David McCullough, *The Path Between the Seas* (New York, 1977), pp. 26-7, reports that "Grant... was indeed the first President to address himself seriously to the [canal] subject... [He] wanted it in the proper place... and he wanted it under American control. 'To Europeans the benefits... of the proposed canal are great,' he was to write, 'to Americans they are incalculable.'" Grant sent seven canal expeditions to Central America between 1870 and 1875. And his connection to the Isthmus did not cease when he left the White House. In John Y. Simon, ed., *The Personal Memoirs of Julia Dent Grant* (New York, 1975), p. 322., Julia recalls that in 1880 Grant "was offered the presidency of the Panama Canal Company in the United States." McCullough records (page 127) that the former president, "flatly declined the offer, a decision Grant explained... 'while I would like to have my name associated with the successful

News of the 4th Infantry's problems on the Isthmus was quick to reach San Francisco. On August 14, the *Daily Alta California* headlined its report that the *Golden Gate* was detained in Panama. The newspaper's great concern was with slow mails and not with casualties; they reported the delay was "on account of the lamentable mismanagement... on the part of the Agent, who had charge of the United States Mails."

Pacific Mail's *Columbia* was the bearer of the news and Captain Call gave a full report when he stepped ashore at San Francisco. The captain told of the *Ohio's* arrival at Aspinwall and how all troops were given sufficient rations to make their way across the Isthmus. "Before arriving at their destinations, the provisions of many failed, when they indulged themselves in eating heartily of all kinds of fruit. The consequence was that many were affected with a species of the cholera... The *Golden Gate* will be detained at Panama until she can obtain a clean bill of health and until the baggage of the troops can be placed on board." The steamship company was not blamed for the delay. The newspaper editorialized: "There is great credit due the Pacific Mail Company for their prompt exertions in relieving and taking care of the sick and suffering."[59] Bonneville's official report supported this conclusion. Almost as an afterthought the names of the Sisters of Charity who died on the Isthmus were published. And Mr. and Mrs. Lynch left three orphans.

Five days later, August 19, the *Daily Alta California* headlined: "Arrival of the *Golden Gate;* Quick Passage

completion of a ship canal between the two oceans, I was not willing to connect it with a failure and one I believe subscribers would lose all they put in.'" Grant turned down the $25,000 salary offer out-of-hand, his annual income at the time was $6,000. But he was right. The Comité Americain, part of Ferdinand de Lessep's ill-fated effort, was a costly failure.

[59] *San Francisco Daily Alta California,* Aug. 14, 1852.

from Panama; Arrival of the 4th Regiment U. S. Infantry;" and, in a feature article entitled, "The Troubles of the *Golden Gate*," told San Francisco the story. Captain C. P. Patterson of the *Golden Gate* reported he was ready for the return trip to California on July 17, but it was the twentieth before 650 of the 4th Infantry arrived. "The remainder of the regiment, some 100 in number, with the sick and camp attendants were received in course of the ensuing week, great delay having occurred in their march over the Isthmus. On the 20th one of the soldiers died of cholera... three more dying the succeeding night." Patterson then repeated the story of the move to the hospital vessel and the apparent checking of the disease, but after July 27, "A change of weather unfortunately caused the cholera to reappear with increased severity, where, with the concurrence of Col. Bonneville, all of the troops were landed upon Flamenco Island. Twenty-nine more soldiers died there along with two crew members while the *Golden Gate* was thoroughly fumigated for several days in succession." Captain Patterson concluded that the deaths were, "solely attributed to the exposure and imprudence of the troops while marching over the Isthmus." The newspaper reported that: "The company certainly did all in their power... and deserve great credit for their prompt and efficient exertions. It is a cause of congratulations for all that the results... were not extended with more disastrous effects." The casualties were noted: "Eighty-four of the troops died... [and] Lieut. Gore... died on board the *Golden Gate*." The story closed with the news that the invalids were left at the island of Flamenco in the Bay of Panama, in charge of Lieuts. Boneycastle, Huger and Surgeon Tripler.[60]

---

[60]*Ibid.*, Aug. 19, 1852.

United States Mail Steamship Company's *Ohio*.
From a lithograph in the Library of Congress.

Pacific Mail Steamship Company's *Golden Gate*.
Reproduced from a copy of a painting by William Marsh in the
Eldredge Collection, Mariners Musuem, Newport News, Virginia.

On August 26, Bonneville submitted his official report on the troop movement from New York to California. He reported the July 5 departure of 651 men, their arrival at Aspinwall, and filled in the details of the disaster with the baggage and cholera. "The Agents having agreed to furnish the troops left behind with everything necessary for their comfort and to transport them to [Benicia, California] as soon as possible, I approved the plan." The 4th's commander summarized his casualties and stated that, "The Agents of the Pacific Mail Steam Ship Company made extraordinary exertions to make the troops comfortable, and subjected themselves to considerable expense in their efforts to administer to the wants of our sick."[61] Not a word for quartermaster Grant who was left on the river to deal with the disaster.

Bonneville's officers did not agree. Hodges called the Pacific Mail management dilatory and incompetent, and the regimental officers formally charged the steamship company with contract failure.

Almost two weeks after the 4th had sailed and was unable to defend itself, the *Panama Herald* thought it had found out who was to blame for the fiasco. On August 17, it published a scathing attack on the officers of the regiment and particularly the quartermaster charging that the troops were:

> Deserted, ...by every commissioned officer,... [while] The officers and their wives came over in the usual time, on mules, in good health and condition. Even the regimental quartermaster, Capt. *GRANT*, could not tarry to attend to his duty, but must come through and await the arrival of the troops on this side!... With Quartermaster *GRANT*, we have not done: Unfitted by either natural ability or education for the post he

---

[61]Lt. Col. B. L. E. Bonneville to Capt. Edward D. Townsend, Aug. 26, 1852, Pacific Division, Letters Received, Record Group 393, Nat. Arch., Wash., D. C.

occupied, he evinced his incapacity at every moment. Totally inefficient himself he left his business to his Sergeant, and then repudiated the expense he had incurred at the Hotel for necessary comfort and attention to sick men, women and children, though promising to settle the account before he left, yet in the end sneaking off on board without even calling at the Hotel to see the bill, and when caught on board the steamer, refusing to pay but a moiety of the expenses ordered by his official![62]

Grant later wrote to Julia that she probably had seen published reports reflecting upon the 4th Infantry officers while crossing the Isthmus and alleging that, "even Capt. Grant ran off and left the men to take care of themselves." He told his wife the story was untrue and that the papers would soon carry the facts.[63]

The indignant 4th Infantry officers' formal resolution of denial appeared in the *San Francisco Herald* on November 1, 1852, and it called the *Panama Herald's* story, "a scandalous and malicious falsehood." The resolutions pointed out that all of the regiment's officers, with three exceptions, stayed with the troops and shared with them the fatigues of the march. The exceptions were one sick officer, the escort for the officers' families, and Captain Grant, who was detained at Cruces to take charge of the baggage. Further, the officers pointed out that Captain Grant was the last officer who left Cruces, he having been obliged to stay there five days in the discharge of his official duties because of the Pacific Mail's failure to provide for the regiment's baggage.[64]

This was Grant's first newspaper controversy and although he was pleased that his fellow officers defended

---

[62]*Grant Association Newsletter* (Jan. 1969) pp. 13-14.
[63]Grant, *Papers*, pp. 270-71.
[64]*Grant Association Newsletter* (Jan. 1969) p. 15.

him, Grant did not publicly say a word on his own behalf, a pattern that he followed invariably.

The *Panama Herald* understandably wanted to place the blame for the disastrous loss of life on the Isthmus on something other than the unhealthy climate or local business interests; the community could lose heavily if the experience of the 4th Infantry influenced future travelers to use other routes to the Pacific Coast.[65]

The charges against Grant were ironic, however, because he probably displayed more personal bravery and calm thinking in the fever-ridden backwater of Cruces than was called for on the major battle fields of the Civil War.[66] And he was never in greater personal danger while serving in the army than during his passage across the Isthmus of Panama in 1852.[67]

---

[65] *Ibid.*, p. 16.
[66] *Ibid.*
[67] *Grant Association Newsletter* (Oct. 1967) p. 1.

Chapter III

California! A Wonderland

In February 1849, Brevet Major General Persifer F. Smith arrived in San Francisco to take command of the new Pacific Division of the Army. Almost at once he began looking for suitable sites to establish his forces.

The leadership of the United States Navy, meanwhile, had been looking for West Coast bases for some time and the ranking Commodore had taken his ship up the great Bay to the two-year-old village of Benicia on the north shore of Carquinez Straits, practically at the mouth of the Sacramento River.[1] He liked what he saw. The Commodore and some of his officers purchased business and house lots in Benicia, but before final arrangements for a navy base could be completed, General Smith marched into town and on April 30, 1849, the army

---

[1] One of the founders of Benicia was General M. G. Vallejo, a handsome soldier from Monterey, who became a member of the State Constitutional Convention, State Senator and Mayor of Sonoma. His wife was Francisca Maria Felipa Benicia. In 1847, when the General deeded five square miles (for $100) of what was to become the new town, he stipulated that it be either Francisca or Benicia. It was first called Francisca, but was changed to avoid confusion with another growing town 30 miles down at the great Bay's entrance which was just then officially switching its name from Yerba Buena to San Francisco.

purchased the eastern edge of the town site that bordered Suisun Bay, thereby pre-empting the navy.[2]

Smith did not like San Francisco because it stuck out like a sore thumb, its climate was troublesome and besides, he reasoned, enemy troops could land easily on the many surrounding beaches.

William Tecumseh Sherman recalled later that a joint Army-Navy Commission selected sites for the permanent federal installations. "After a most careful study," Lieut. Sherman wrote, "Mare Island was selected for the navy-yard and... Benicia for the storehouses and arsenals of the Army." The Pacific Mail Steamship Company, the largest ship company of the day, also selected Benicia for its depot.

At that time Benicia and San Francisco were locked in a struggle to become what young Sherman dubbed, "The future city of the Pacific." Sherman went on to report: "General Smith, being disinterested and unprejudiced, decided on Benicia as the point where the city ought to be, and where Army headquarters should be."[3]

In early 1849, after a considerable amount of "arm twisting" by local citizens, General Smith founded his new installation on about 100 acres. Two companies of the 2nd Infantry arrived, barracks and storehouses were constructed and the army was in business at Benicia Barracks. Later, Army headquarters in Washington accepted his recommendation to move Pacific Division

[2] This area — first called Benicia Barracks and later Benicia Arsenal — remained in army hands 115 years until 1964 when it was deactivated and the land purchased by the City of Benicia. The navy slipped back about eight miles into upper San Pablo Bay, bought Mare Island and has been there ever since.

[3] Sherman spent ten years of the formative period of his life in California and was at Benicia much longer than Grant. Sherman surveyed some of the area around Benicia and left his name on at least one island. These quotations are from William T. Sherman, *Recollections of California, 1846-1861* (Oakland, 1945).

supply headquarters from San Francisco, and a small ordnance company was ordered from Fort Monroe, Virginia, to set up the California Ordnance Department next to the Barracks. This became Benicia Arsenal.

The original Benicia Arsenal Log's first entry, dated January 13, 1851, at Fort Monroe, Virginia, noted the formation of the "California Company" with 19 men. After sailing on the transport ship *Helen McGraw* around the Horn, the first entry at Benicia of the now-called California Ordnance Depot was made September 5, 1851; Brevet Captain Charles P. Stone commander. The organization called itself Benicia Arsenal for the first time in its entry of April 12, 1851.[4]

Since it was the army's principal arsenal on the Pacific Coast, the facility was built to last. Huge sandstone blocks were cut by workmen at quarries in the nearby hills and permanent buildings, some with four-foot thick walls, were erected. The army brought in skilled stone cutters from the East and some of their work still commands respect.

Many of these original buildings not only stand today in remarkably good condition, but they are believed to be some of the finest examples of the stonecutters art remaining in California.[5] Two Benicia warehouses completed in 1853-1854 were of this finely-crafted native stone. They still exist and today are called the "camel barns" because during a brief period during the

[4] *Log of Ordnance Company at Benicia Arsenal, January 13, 1851-March 25, 1869;* the original arsenal log was purchased by the Benicia Historical Society in 1976. The writer was privileged to study the log before it became available to the public.
[5] The original arsenal building, construction beginning in 1851, blew up in 1912 in "one of the most spectacular fires ever witnessed on the coast . . .," full of ammunition, the explosion sent red hot pieces sailing through the air for considerable distances. When the army rebuilt, they made the old building two stories instead of the original four. Marguerite Hunt, *History of Solano County* (Chicago; 1926).

Civil War they were used to stable camels that were imported by the army in an experiment to improve transportation in the desert west.

When gold was discovered, Benicia became an important way station because the nearest route to the gold fields from the outside world was up the Bay into the Sacramento River. Seagoing vessels could sail to Benicia where smaller steamboats went up the river. Also, a four-mule overland stage ran between Benicia and Sacramento.

Benicia was well-sited on the shore of Carquinez Straits with a magnificent view across the water to gently rolling hills and Mount Diablo. With a mild and pleasant climate, and located at the head of ocean navigation, Benicia was in a position to command the trade of California interior rivers and valleys. For a time Benicia threatened to outstrip San Francisco as the leading city in Northern California.[6]

Benicia and Monterey were the initial towns incorporated under the first California legislature in early 1850. Benicia became the first education center of California with several schools for young ladies, and the home of the State's first Protestant Church. Benicia activity focused on the Arsenal and many social events were held there with army and town folks in attendance. Benicia, in Solano County, became California's capital in February 1853, when the State legislature moved there (a seventh relocation). But on the last day of February 1854, the Government departed — ledger, file and bureaucrat — for Sacramento, never to move again.

Solano County, one of the 27 original California counties, received its name indirectly from a missionary priest, Father Francisco Solano, who gave his name in baptism to the chief of one of the region's Indian tribes.

---

[6]"Benicia State House," Calif. Hist. Qtly., Vol. 17 (1938), p. 261.

General M. G. Vallejo, the most respected Californio landowner, requested that the county be named in honor of Chief Solano who fought with Vallejo in earlier Indian wars. After losing its place as California's capital, Benicia slipped further when the county seat was moved to Fairfield in 1858.[7]

But the proud little town was a thriving community in the early 1850s, the establishment of the federal base having made it so. During that time Benicia was the gathering place for much of northern California's society, and the Arsenal played a significant role in the social life.[8]

It was into this scene that the 4th Infantry came, worn and sick from its Isthmus ordeal, when the *Golden Gate* dropped anchor in August 1852. But, with a young man's bounce, U. S. Grant put the just-completed, hazardous trip behind him, and looked to the days ahead. "We are going to a fine country," he wrote Julia as the *Golden Gate* steamed north from San Diego, "and a new one, with great prospects... Chances must arrise... to make something [for us, or] at least be something for our children." The only blot on his high hopes was the separation from his family and the lack of contact. "If I could only know that you three are well I would be perfectly satisfied with my position."[9]

As he looked at the peaceful but barren land around

---

[7]Fairfield-Suisun Chamber of Commerce, *"INFO-MAP,"* 1975.

[8]Background material on Benicia is from Marguerite Hunt, *op. cit.;* "An Historical View of the former Benicia Military Arsenal," a pamphlet printed by Benicia Industries, Inc., 1975; *Benicia's Early Glory,* a 111 page booklet published by the Solano County Hist. Soc., 1958; *History of Solano and Napa Counties* by Tom Gregory, 1912; *History of Solano County,* edited by J.P. Munro Fraser, 1879; Josephine W. Cowell's *History of Benicia Arsenal,* 1963; Jacqueline M. Woodruff's *Benicia, The Promise of California,* 1947; *Great Expectations: The Story of Benicia, California,* Richard H. Dillon, 1981; and the unselfish help of history buffs associated with The Benicia Historical Society, Solano County Historical Society, Benicia City Library, Benicia Industries, Inc., and the Benicia Chamber of Commerce.

[9]Grant, *Papers,* p. 255.

him, Grant was sure that the troops would recover the health and weight that most had lost on the Isthmus crossing. He thought himself down to jockey-size — "prime order," he said, for "doing anything where a light weight was required." Grant weighed less than 135 pounds at that time. He summed up his impressions of his new, temporary station with the observation, "Benicia is a nice, healthy place."[10]

Grant could never accept the high cost of living in California. "At Benicia in 1852," he observed, "flour was 25 cents per pound; potatoes were 16 cents... onions 37½ cents." A cook could not be hired for army captain's pay. And it was impossible, he pointed out, for officers to survive if they had not been allowed to buy from commissary supplies at New Orleans wholesale prices.[11]

But despite California's outrageous prices, U.S. Grant was sincerely attracted to the new land. "I have seen enough," he wrote from Benicia, "to know that it is a different country from any thing a person in the states could imagine in their wildest dreams. There is no reason why an active, energetic person should not make a fortune every year." In his first letter from Benicia he enthused to Julia, "I could quit the Army to-day and in one year go home with enough to make us comfortable, on Gravois, all our life." But then his more cautious nature caused him to add — "Of course I do not contemplate doing any such thing of the sort, because what I have is a certainty, and what I might expect to do, might prove a dream."[12]

Quickly moving in with Brevet Captain Frederick Steele, a classmate who had attended his wedding, Grant could hardly wait to get going and to move around after his long shipboard confinement. After being introduced

[10]*Ibid.*, p. 256.   [11]Grant, *Memoirs*, p. 203.   [12]Grant, *Papers*, p. 257.

to San Francisco, he was excited about seeing more of California and anxious to visit Julia's brother, John Dent, who was in business and mining on the Stanislaus River near the foothills of the Sierra Nevada.

Saturday, the 21st of August, in the cool of the evening with the never-ceasing breeze in his face, Grant boarded the new mail steamer *Sophie* a few hours out of San Francisco, bound upriver for Stockton.[13] He was keyed-up for his first trip away from the California coast and looking forward to seeing his in-laws, the Dent brothers. These small steamers were so crowded that berths and even seats were out of the question. Passengers slept where they could, bothered all night with mosquitoes, flies, fleas and bedbugs.[14]

Almost everything used by the villages and mines of the southern Sierra came by boat to Stockton, was loaded there on pack mules or large freight wagons for the journey to Knight's Ferry and on to Sonora, Chinese Camp, Big Oak Flat, and the other southern mines. The freight route to the fabulous southern mines of the Mother Lode started at the loading levee at Stockton.

Everything was dumped on the levee in heaps that eventually were sorted out, packed up and hauled off to the mines. As early as 1849 freight wagons began to take the place of the pack trains, the county being flat to the foothills. By 1851 some 500 wagons and 1,500 mules were shuttling back and forth along the freight route.

---

[13] At least eight small steamers plied between San Francisco and Stockton during 1852. In the summer of that year only three were advertised as making regularly scheduled trips: *H. T. Clay, American Eagle,* and *Sophie.* From a study of schedules and contemporary newspapers, the author has concluded that Grant made his trip from Benicia to Stockton in 1852 on the *Sophie. The San Francisco Daily Herald,* May 5, 1852; *San Joaquin Republican,* Feb. 11, 1852, June 30, 1852, and Sept. 1, 1852.

[14] Hinton R. Helper, "The Land of Gold" quoted in V. Covert Martin, *Stockton Album: Through the Years* (Stockton, 1959), p. 76.

Stage lines started, mail was delivered by contract, and thousands of tons of goods were transported annually through Knight's Ferry. Stockton's miner's road went straight east from the levee area; tents and traveling men lined the road all the way out of town. At night camp fires dotted the entire distance from Stockton to Knight's Ferry. There was a continuous procession of men and pack animals plodding along. The traffic was considered as heavy as any place in the United States.[15]

The clattering wagons, pulled by horses or mules and driven by shouting and swearing teamsters, moved slowly out of Stockton down Weber, Pilgrim, Main Street and Wilson Way to the Mariposa Military Road and the Sonora Road, which were the same until they split just east of what is now the fair grounds; here the Sonora Road went on toward Farmington. Pack animals carried about 300 pounds each. Freight animals could pull 1,500-2,000 pounds depending on the surface of the road.[16]

Arriving in Stockton just before dawn, a little more rumpled than usual from being stretched out on *Sophie's* benches, Grant got off on the levee, strolled down Weber's Avenue, not yet planked, to a livery stable where he woke up the owner and made a deal to "rent" a mule for the ride to Knight's Ferry. Heading out Miners Avenue crossing José Jesus Street (renamed "Grant" years later) directly east of the Stockton-Sonora Road, Grant angled down to Boston House, crossed French Camp Creek to 16 Mile House and Oregon Ranch and then drifted southeast, crossing Littlejohn's Creek on

[15]Irene D. Paden and Margaret E. Schlichtman, *The Big Oak Flat Road* (San Francisco, 1955), pp. 15-19.
[16]*Ibid.*

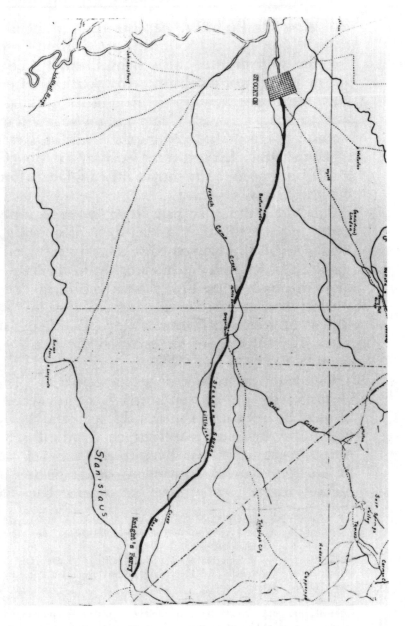

Map of a Portion of the Gold Mining Region of California.
Stockton-Knight's Ferry route is highlighted.
Owen C. Coy, California Historical Association, 1948.

into Knight's Ferry.[17] The distance was about forty miles.[18]

Grant was surprised to see houses almost every mile and to find the road much more crowded than those in the East. Jammed with wagons, lurching and rocking their way to Sonora, Angels Camp and the southern mines, almost all of the traffic crossing the Stanislaus River had to use the Dent's ferry. It was a hard day's ride but Grant arrived in time for a late supper at Lewis Dent's home in Knight's Ferry.

The hamlet that Capt. Sam Grant saw as he turned the corner of Sonora Road (now called Grant Street) was the kind of a town that blossomed in its first twenty years and withered for the next one hundred. A small village along the north bank of the Stanislaus River, Knight's Ferry stuck stubbornly to the side of a steep, little hill. Ranch land and the cemetery were at the top; the long narrow main street at the bottom matched the river's gentle meanderings.[19]

One block up from Main, at the corner of Ellen and Dean Streets, stood the Lewis Dent residence (the "Long" house) with its ancient fig tree in the back yard. Even today the house is still attractive and still rich with memories of those who lived there. One still can see "L.Dent" scratched on a window pane at the back of the home. George Dent's home, its original lines hardly

---

[17]"Map of a Portion of the Gold Mining Region of California" by Owen C. Coy, Calif. State Hist. Assoc., 1948. Also "Map of the Southern Mines," by C. D. Gibbes, 1852. Lithograph of Quirot & Co.

[18]Stockton Directory of Emigrant's Guide To Southern Mines. "Table of Distances," p. 45 courtesy of Anna Angelini, Ref. Dept. Stockton-San Joaquin Co. Pub. Lby., Nov. 24, 1976 letter to the author.

[19]John F. Criswell, Knight's Ferry's Golden Past (Oakdale, Cal., 1972). Mr. Criswell's little book is a "gold mine" of information, and the best publication on this fascinating piece of California history. The author gratefully acknowledges Mr. Criswell's assistance through interviews and correspondence.

recognizable, is behind the old Masonic Hall which is empty now, but once was the site of Stanislaus County Courthouse.

Of course, the river made the town (the railroad never came in spite of heavy, local pressures), and periodically the river would remind frail humanity who was boss. Floods were recorded at various times from 1849 to 1965. The big flood was in 1862 when the river rose to a depth of 40 feet and became 300 feet wide. Fires, also, severely damaged Knight's Ferry through the years and helped discourage further growth.

In the early and mid-1850s Indians lived near the town. They dug for gold dust and stole horses, but otherwise were not troublesome.

The Stanislaus River rises in the Sierra, runs westward to the San Joaquin Valley and joins with other streams that fall eventually into San Francisco Bay. The upper part of the river slips through canyons and gorges that prevent easy crossing. At the point where Knight's Ferry sits the Stanislaus pushes out of the foothills, loses force, and becomes a ladylike stream; it is about the nearest point to the mountains where crossing becomes practical.

A hot-tempered native of Indiana, Dr. William Knight came to this picturesque spot in the early 1840s and was impressed with the natural crossing. He recognized it as the most direct path between the flat valley and the southern Sierra. When gold fever struck and prospectors moved inland, Knight, who had settled above Sacramento, headed back to the crossing he was certain would be on the main route to the developing mines at Angels Camp and Sonora. His foresight proved to be accurate.

With his associate, Captain Vantine, Knight made the first permanent camp. In a few months the two partners had the beginnings of a hotel, a trading post and a ferry service. Things were going well until November 1849 when William Knight, ever argumentative, was killed in a shoot-out on the main street. Captain Vantine was left to carry on the new businesses alone.

In 1850 John and Lewis Dent passed through Knight's Ferry. They came to California by ox-team from St. Louis in 1849, moving West to seek a fortune. Both impressive looking, the tall young men were well-educated and natural-born leaders. Lewis, the younger, was a lawyer and had been elected a delegate to California's constitutional convention at age 26. Thirty-four-year-old John was a solid citizen of imagination and sound judgement. Right away the Dents saw opportunity at Knight's Ferry so they "threw in" with Vantine, bought out the holdings of Knight's estate, and began to develop the area.

The three partners built the ferry, while establishing and expanding the tavern, trading post, restaurant, stables, and supporting services. The Dents later added a fair-sized ranch at the top of the hill and still later constructed a northside ditch to provide water, first for mining use and then for household and gardens. On one day in 1850 it was recorded that more than 100 heavily loaded wagon freighters crossed south on the ferry headed for the mines.[20]

President Buchanan named John the Indian Agent for the Wallas who lived upstream about a mile. Lewis became justice of the peace and owner of the nicest house in town.

In early March 1852, after days of torrential rains, the river overflowed its banks up to the town and created

---

[20] *Stockton Argus* newspaper report quoted in Paden and Schlichtman, *op. cit.*, p. 22.

KNIGHT'S FERRY,

ON THE

Stanislaus River.

——o——

DENT, VANTINE & CO.,

HAVE the best and most frequented ferry on the Stanislaus. It is preëminently the

SUMMER CROSSING.

It requires no puffing, inasmuch as *all* cross here who go to Sonora, or any of the Stanislaus, Tuolumne or Merced Diggings. It is thirty-five miles from Stockton, and about twenty-eight to Sonora. The road has been travelled by so many thousands, and so many thousands of dollars spent on its improvement, that it is easier for the traveller than any other road in the country.

A TWO STORY BUILDING

has been erected at the ferry, for the accommodation of the travelling public. The table cannot be surpassed by any on the road; and in the bar may be found the best wine, liquor and cigars the country affords. Feed for animals constantly on hand. Terms reasonable.

Advertisement in *The Stockton Directory and Emigrant's Guide to the Southern Mines.*
Published by the "San Joaquin Republican" in 1852.

havoc all the way down to the broad valley. Every ferry on the Stanislaus was swept away except the one at Knight's Ferry which, due to the vigilance of the Dents, remained in business and was the only one operating for several months. That summer, after the flood, and just before brother-in-law Ulysses' first visit, the Dents bought out Vantine and secured control of virtually every business activity in town.

John moved swiftly to have the town surveyed, recorded, and officially named "Dentville" in preparation for the population expansion he saw coming. The name never caught on — travelers insisted on calling the place Knight's Crossing or Knight's Ferry. John laid out the streets and sold or gave away lots until there were 800 persons living there. In late 1852, 32-year-old George, the third Dent brother, moved to Knight's Ferry with his family. He became postmaster in 1855.

New businesses, including a flour mill and a saw mill, added to traffic until the ferry was being backed up enough to cause grumbling among its customers. This led to the development of a competitor upriver at Two-Mile Bar: the Dent's countered this move with the purchase of the next down river ferry.

After Grant returned to Missouri, gold was discovered on the banks of the Stanislaus near Knight's Ferry and the town boomed again with house lots selling as high as $2,000 each. Every canyon and gulch was worked, some by the Chinese who were paid 25¢ a day by the miners. But the Dents, on November 1, 1856, tiring of their enterprises, sold out.

Lewis moved later to Stockton to open a law practice, but John stayed at Knight's Ferry until 1862 when he returned East.

Grant found the Dent brothers the first citizens of Knight's Ferry and proprietors of a thriving business netting up to one hundred dollars a day. He wrote Julia that there were three daily stages carrying eight to twelve passengers crossing both ways on the ferry with everybody stopping at Knight's Ferry House, a tavern owned by the Dent's, to eat one dollar dinners. "They have stables rented to the stage companies for almost two hundred dollars a month, board for the teamsters at ten dollars per week and a trading post, where they get pretty much all the dust the Indians and some miners dig," he reported to Julia. In addition, Grant wrote, they had a ranch with several hundred head of cattle and numerous horses, "all worth about thribble what they would be in the Atlantic States."[21]

The ferry crossing the 150 foot river held Grant's interest closely. He found it operated by two men who pulled it across with ropes attached to each shore. It took only about one minute to cross, but the ride cost two dollars.

Captain Sam stayed with Lewis Dent and was most impressed with the house. He enjoyed the front view of the river and the hills as he gazed south, but he enjoyed particularly sitting on the low and long back porch, which was snuggled against the hill side, feet up on the railing, smoking and chatting with John. Things did not seem so lonely and Julia did not seem quite so far away as the men talked of home and the strange new world in which they found themselves. Gold, money, and opportunities to make more, dominated much of the conversation.

Grant relished his week at Knight's Ferry: he watched the Indians, enjoyed seeing the ferry's cable and current

---

[21]Grant, *Papers*, p. 259.

propulsion, hiked and rode up in the foothills to the mines, and talked with the miners. But most of all, like the residents in town, he delighted in meeting the stage. When the stage arrived in a cloud of dust everybody turned out to see who got off and to get the news.

Grant wanted to be in Benicia on Monday morning, anxious to straighten out administrative problems remaining from the Panama crossing, so he had to start back on Sunday morning. He and John, not knowing how long it would be before they saw each other again, stayed up almost all Saturday night talking. When at last they did lie down for an hour or so, Grant found himself the target of an angry army of ants that drove him from his bed. He wrote Julia, in his characteristic colorful but carefree style, "I got awake finding myself covered with a meriad of Aunts."[22]

Thus with reluctance, on Sunday the 29th, Grant departed from Knight's Ferry before 8:00 a.m., reaching Stockton before 3:00 p.m. that afternoon. This return trip was faster and more pleasant for two reasons; Grant was on a horse instead of a mule, and at the last minute, John Dent decided to accompany him back to Benicia.

Grant and John boarded the steamer in Stockton almost immediately upon their arrival. With numerous delays, they reached Benicia at dawn, although they had been scheduled in at midnight. With very little sleep for two nights Grant was one tired soldier during that day, but delighted to receive three letters from "the states." It was a disappointment however that Julia's letter had been forwarded from Governors Island, New York, before she knew that he had departed. So he still knew nothing of her condition or that of the expected baby.

---

[22]*Ibid.*, p. 260.

By the time Grant returned from Knight's Ferry the 4th Infantry had organized itself, was under tent, and camped on the bluff above the permanent buildings of the post. Ulysses wrote to his wife that he "was highly delighted with evrything I saw" in California and wanted to see as much as possible before departing for Fort Vancouver.[23]

When former President Grant toured interior California in 1879 he and Mrs. Grant were honored guests at a large reception in Stockton. Stockton's *Daily Evening Herald* reported that "Grant's speech was principally a denial of the various reports . . . about his having lived at Knight's Ferry in the early days. There are men about Knight's Ferry who claim to have a distinct recollection of playing seven-up with Grant, and indulging in other frontier pastimes away back twenty-five or thirty years ago." They might have done so, but that would have been possible only during his brief visits.

The newspaper reported that in his short response Grant spoke substantially as follows:

> I have been in Stockton before, having passed through here six times, but this is the longest time I have ever spent here, and the first time I have ever been inside a house in your city . . . I have to-day met several persons who claimed to have known me in Knight's Ferry in 1849. As I was never west of the Rocky Mountains excepting as a soldier in the Mexican War, until 1852, I think I must have been personated on this coast by some other person. I was at Knight's Ferry three times — once 1852, once in 1853 and once in 1854, and I think I never remained there at any time longer than one week. The parties who think that they have known me at that place must, therefore, have been mistaken. I am, however, pleased that hereafter I can truly say that I have been in Stockton . . .[24]

[23]*Ibid.*, p. 266.   [24]*Stockton Daily Evening Herald*, Oct. 1, 1879.

Grant was a little miffed with all the stories and misunderstandings about his time in interior California. His biographers have repeated stories about him which were fanciful, exaggerated, and untrue. He resented their implications. When U. S. Grant became a well-known figure in the early 1860s, and later as he earned the status of national hero, it was perhaps natural that a series of myths about his West Coast service would develop. Some of them are ludicrous, some insulting and a few are even humorous. For example:

> In the Hoopa Valley in the redwood forests of Northern California the remains of Fort Gaston are near the Trinity River. The U. S. Grant house there was supposedly used by the young Captain for a short time in 1850's. Since Gaston was not established until 1858 Grant could not have stayed there.[25]

A Grass Valley, California, Clergyman, R. F. Putnam, touring the state in 1863 recorded the following in his diary:

> We reached Knight's Ferry, distance about 40 miles from Stockton at 12:00 o'clock ... General Grant spent a winter at Knight's Ferry. He had a cabin in the hillside not far from the hotel. To my inquiry of the landlord, what did the General do while here, the reply was, 'He did nothing but drink whiskey and get tight.'[26]

Robert A. Curtin, an old California pioneer, wrote autobiographical notes which he gave to Margaret E. Schlichtman in 1950, brimful of early California anecdotes. Curtin observed:

> There is no doubt that U. S. Grant lived at Knight's Ferry and later was transferred to Eureka as just below that city is Fort

---

[25]Herbert M. Hart, *Old Forts of the Northwest* (Seattle, 1965), p. 39.
[26]R. F. Putnam Journal, 1863, pp. 263-64. The original manuscript of his journal is owned by the Calif. Hist. Soc., San Francisco.

Lewis Dent residence in Knight's Ferry,
where Grant stayed during his visits.

Historical Marker near Knight's Ferry.
This bridge was constructed in 1863 after the
disastrous flood of 1861. The Dents and Grant
had long been gone from the area when
this bridge was designed and built.

Grant now used as a warehouse. Many old settlers and ranchers who lived around there and knew him were living in my time... Grant's camp at Knight's Ferry was on the south side of the river on a spot below the bridge where the ranch home of Jimmy Slone was built. I believe the old oak tree still stands where his camp was. His father-in-law, Dent had a ferry boat there and it has been said that Grant drew up plans for the bridge.[27]

A *San Francisco Chronicle* story had Grant meeting Julia Dent at Knight's Ferry:

Quite a few families had established themselves at the river crossing among them being the Dents. As there was a big Indian camp there just back of where the Grayson Hotel stands, and with the on rush of the people coming to the mines, fear of trouble with them, the Territorial Governor had an army post placed there. U. S. Grant was the Commander. It was he no doubt who drew up the plans for the present covered bridge. For many years a big cannon mounted on wheels stood by the flour mill, no doubt left there when the army post was abandoned. As General Grant's wife was Julia Dent, there is no doubt that while on his detail there is where he became acquainted with the Dent Family.[28]

Captain Grant had spent a few hours in San Francisco before arriving at Benicia, had been amazed at what he saw, and wanted to see more. During the last week of August 1852, he took the steamer down to spend a few more days at the city, and he wrote to Julia that he considered San Francisco "the wonder of the world."[29]

Placer mining for gold was at its height, and San Francisco was a focal point — steamboats departing for and returning from Stockton and Sacramento every

[27]Robert A. Curtin, autobiographical notes in Margaret E. Schlichtman papers, the Bancroft Lby., Berkeley, Calif., Univ. of Calif.

[28]*San Francisco Chronicle*, clipping, date uncertain.

[29]Grant, *Papers*, p. 266.

evening; riotous living and easy spending were the trademarks of the time. San Francisco wharves were packed with crowds of people shouting, pushing and shoving to meet the miners from both the northern and southern mines who came, as Grant said, to "sell their dust and to have a time."[30] Some of the greeters were "runners" from hotels and restaurants who shouted out their sponsors and grabbed at the miners. Grant observed that others were "adventurers, of good manners and good presence, . . . young men of good family, good education and gentlemanly instincts," who were on the alert to meet debarking passengers of ready means.[31]

In later years Grant recalled that many of the scenes in the California life he saw, "exceed in strangeness and interest any of the mere products from the brain of the novelist." And all of it unfolded before his eyes.[32]

Everybody thought one could pick up fortunes without effort, he wrote. Some adventurers did exceed their wildest expectations, but for every one that struck it rich, Grant thought, there were hundreds who failed — many filling unknown graves. "Those early days in California brought out character," he observed.[33] It was a young man's country in the fall of 1852, but Grant saw that many a young man became dismayed and not a few "without vicious instinct, became criminals and outcasts."[34] Others took off their coats and looked for a job although many had studied professions and had never done a day's manual labor in their lives. This was the kaleidoscope that the newcomer saw as his active West Coast duty began — a picture that stayed fresh in his memory for over thirty, eventful years.

Ulysses wrote Julia that San Francisco, although only

[30]Grant, *Memoirs*, p. 200.
[31]*Ibid.*   [32]*Ibid.*, p. 201.   [33]*Ibid.*   [34]*Ibid.*

settled for a few years "contains a wealthy population of probably fifty thousand persons." He was amazed to see such vigorous 'growth in a city that had burned three times and had been rebuilt each time better than before. Grant noted that homes were either built on ground that had been created by fill or where the hills had been dug away. And, ever the practical quartermaster, he reported that the labor cost "not less than five dollars per day."[35]

All during Grant's sojourn on the West Coast, gold and its rowdy influence on California economics was the important fact of life. California underwent extraordinary development between 1848 and the start of the Civil War, and gold played a major role in that development. Production began in late January 1848, when gold was discovered on the American River. For some time during that year news of the strike did not leak out and production was small. A few hardy San Franciscans took off for the interior, but the uncomfortable trip into the hills in hot and dry weather discouraged most citizens. By November 1848, however, the small group that kept working were sending back appreciable amounts of gold dust to San Francisco.

It was between 1850 and 1853 that the gold industry really began to boom. Gold production grew rapidly and transportation to the East was constantly being improved. Refiners and assayers set up shop in San Francisco, Sacramento, and other towns. The population swelled in 1850, in late 1852, and again in early 1853. (At times during 1851, however, there were more people going out of California than coming in, partly because of the Australian gold strike.)[36]

---

[35]Grant, *Papers*, p. 266.

[36]This material on gold and California economics comes from the scholarly article: Thomas Senior Berry, "Gold! But How Much?," *Calif. Hist. Qtly.*, Fall, 1976.

Much has been made of Grant's well-recorded string of business failures on the West Coast, but they were not unique. In the early to mid-1850s business life in remote California was strictly boom and bust. Particularly in San Francisco, trading center for the ill-equipped miners and the growing population, was this true. Market demands were so fierce that opportunities for profit were everywhere. As it turned out, however, the significant profits went to the very few who had solid East Coast mercantile connections and reasonably good fortune with the unreliable shippers.

Also necessary for business survival in this "harum-scarum" atmosphere was staying ability. The ability to survive severe financial stresses, hard-driving competition, and less than honest city authorities, was necessary in California business life in the early 1850s.

The shipping companies were known best for damaged goods and poor service, and customers seemed skilled in non-payment of bills. These were unique times and most San Francisco businessmen lived on the ragged edge of failure. Everybody tried everything. One merchant wrote, "In a new country a man must be ready to jump at everything that could be done with honour . . . It would be hard to say who will be good & who insolvent here, in the course of three months."[37]

Pricing, return on investment, and inventory positions were difficult to determine. In a matter of months between 1850 and 1852, building materials — bricks, lime, etc. — almost doubled in price. Potatoes doubled in price during a two-week period in November-December 1852. Real estate developments buzzed along at a high

[37] This quotation, and material on San Francisco business practices, is from James W. White, "Great Expectations: The Business Correspondence of 'Gibbons & Lammot,' Gold Rush Black Powder Merchants," *Calif. Hist. Qtly.*, Winter, 1976.

pace. From July 1852, to January 1853, one San Francisco business lot went from $1,500 to $4,500 in price. In a few months during 1853 house lots that were out of town almost overnight became covered with commercial buildings.

Military officers were allowed to "moonlight" in those years and most army and navy men with money or credit spent countless hours attempting to better themselves financially. Army doctors had civilian practices on the side, military lawyers the same. Investments, rightly called "speculations," were the main topic of conversation and a principal driving force of military people caught in the inflationary California society of the 1850s.

Returning to Benicia from his San Francisco visits, Grant continued his tour of northern California and spent the bright, late summer days galloping over the countryside looking at its "resources." "The whole country from Benicia to the southern limits of the state, where not cultivated, abounds with... luxuriant growth..."[38]

One of his side trips took him to Vallejo, which Grant found cheerless and dreary. Although it had been the State Capital for eight months, it was a desolate, windswept town. There were few adequate houses, restaurants, or even laundry facilities — and, important to soldiers on leave, entertainment was practically nonexistent. The streets were mud holes following a rain, and the yelping coyotes kept the town folk awake all night. It would be no wonder if Grant headed north for Sonoma which had a reputation for good company and better times.

According to Vallejo family tradition, Grant rode to Sonoma where he met the most noble Californian of them

[38]Grant, *Papers*, p. 266.

all, General M. G. Vallejo. There is doubt that the meeting ever took place, but its telling adds romance to Grant's life in pioneer California.

The sunny hills and attractive valleys around Sonoma provided a proper setting for the amiable Californio who was the centerpiece of California activity for twenty years before a fickle fate turned against him. Mariano Guadalupe Vallejo was the well-respected commander of California's northern frontier in Mexican days who found himself at the hub of international power politics when the ambitions of Spain, Russia, Mexico, England and the United States clashed over California's future.

From the 1830s General Vallejo's life mirrored California's transition from a Hispanic to an Anglo culture. He steered events which carried him upward to great wealth and power. Later, he was to suffer obscurity and financial disaster, but he never lost his gentlemanly bearing, his love for California, nor the respect of those who knew him.

As an increasing number of Americans poured into the Golden State in the 1840s, General Vallejo concluded that a takeover by the United States was inevitable. He embraced America and became a loyal and leading citizen. He was a delegate to California's constitutional convention, a state senator, the mayor of Sonoma, and he donated, or sold for a pittance, great tracts of land which became the towns of Vallejo, Sonoma and Benicia, among others.[39]

---

[39]General background of Vallejo from State of California, *Sonoma State Historical Park*, (Sacramento: Dept. of Parks and Recreation, undated); Myrtle M. McKittrick, *Vallejo, Son of California* (Portland; 1944); Henry D. Hubbard, *Vallejo* (Boston; 1941); Leonard Pitt, *The Decline of the Californios* (Berkeley; 1966); George D. Lyman, "First Native-Born California Physician," *Calif. Hist. Soc. Qtly.*, Sept., 1925; George Tays, "Mariano Guadalupe Vallejo and Sonoma," *Calif. Hist. Soc. Qtly.*, Vol. 17, 1938; and Emparan, cited below.

General Vallejo's home in Sonoma, less than thirty miles from the capital city that bore his name, was always open to the American officers. They took great delight in Vallejo's family, his inspired dinners (he had the only French chef in that part of California) and the sport and activity that centered about him. Sonoma was the site of an active army camp in California between 1849 and late 1851, which made it a natural stopover for the officers who found a lively and entertaining oasis in what otherwise was almost a cultural desert.

William Tecumseh Sherman documents two of his visits to the Vallejo home in his writings. Lieutenant Henry W. Halleck was a great admirer of the California general. Joseph Hooker lived ten years as a neighbor and Philip H. Sheridan became acquainted with the general and corresponded with Vallejo years later. Even the navy was represented at the Vallejo home as Captain Farragut, commanding officer of Mare Island (named for one of Vallejo's lost horses), and his wife became close friends of both Senora de Vallejo and her courtly husband. Vallejo spoke passable English but his wife did not.

His first home in Sonoma, "La Casa Grande," was one of the most imposing and well-furnished private residences in California. The large adobe house stood on the north side of Sonoma's central plaza and welcomed a steady stream of distinguished visitors from all over the world during the decade of 1840. It was at La Casa Grande in June 1846, where General Vallejo was taken prisoner by the Bear Flag revolutionaries.

In 1851-1852 the Vallejos completed their new and even grander home, "Lachryma Montis" (Mountain Tear), where they resided for more than 35 years through the wealthy days and poverty years that followed.

Vallejo family tradition has it that the distinguished general met Captain Grant in California and, indeed, entertained young Grant at his Sonoma home in the early 1850s. Further, the tale continues, the elderly general journeyed "back East" during the Civil War, saw Commanding General Grant and renewed their acquaintanceship. Most of the "evidence" concerning the friendship of these two famous personages had its foundation with recollections of Dr. Planton M. G. Vallejo, the general's son and the first native California physician. Dr. Vallejo stated unequivocally that Grant had been a guest and "royally entertained at Lachryma Montis." Based on Planton's faulty memory, the myth of this friendship endured.[40]

Several biographers of Vallejo, using the same source — Planton Vallejo's memoirs — incorrectly tied young Grant to the famous general. George D. Lyman, Myrtle Garrison, Harry D. Hubbard and Myrtle M. McKittrick made the same mistake. Garrison wrote:

> Here it was [at Vallejo's home] that General Vallejo entertained all notables who happened to visit California. Among his visitors, following the war between Mexico and the United States, were Generals Sherman, Sheridan and Grant.[41]

The local newspaper joined in the chorus:

> When Sonoma was a military post — July 1846 to the end of 1851 — many young army officers were stationed here for periods of time. Many of them later became high-ranking officers and won fame in the Civil War. Among them were Ulysses S. Grant...[42]

---

[40]Planton Vallejo, "Memories of the Vallejos," San Francisco Bulletin, Feb. 14, 1914. Also, William M. Roberts, the Bancroft Library, to the author, Jan. 14, 1977.
[41]Myrtle Garrison, Romance and History of California Ranchos, (San Francisco; 1935), pp. 64-65.
[42]Sonoma Index-Tribune, 1968, Vol. 89, No. 16.

There is authoritative opinion that Grant and Vallejo did not meet, specifically in California, and never knew each other. Robert D. Parmelee, prominent Sonoma attorney and historian investigated this subject carefully and convinced himself that no meeting ever took place. He wrote in 1976: "I have no reliable record to indicate that Grant was ever in Sonoma or that he met the Vallejo Family.... Planton's recollections are entirely unreliable."[43]

A Bancroft Library researcher at the University of California in Berkeley answered a query in 1976:

> I am unable to substantiate by direct evidence that Vallejo and Grant met here in the early 1850s. Vallejo's own memoirs cover the period up to 1849; his correspondence covers later years, but there are no letters either to or from Grant in the period 1852 to 1854. I was able to glance at some of Vallejo's correspondence, but I could find no mention of Grant.[44]

The writer's study of Grant's *Memoirs* and the Grant *Papers* does not connect the two. His research on the subject at the Henry E. Huntington Library, Sonoma Public Library, the Bancroft Library, and his field research in Sonoma, Vallejo and Solano County had the same negative results.

Parmelee's *Pioneer Sonoma,* published in 1972, has the best listing of future federal generals who were stationed in Sonoma between 1849 and 1852.

	Civil War Grade
William Tecumseh Sherman	Major General
Joseph Hooker	Major General
George Stoneman	Major General
Alfred Biggs	Major General

[43]Robert D. Parmelee to the author, Nov. 8, 1976.
[44]William M. Roberts to the author, Dec. 7, 1976.

Andrew J. Smith	Major General
Alfred Pleasonton	Major General
Frederick Steele	Major General
John W. Davidson	Major General
Philip Kearny	Major General
Charles P. Stone	Brigadier General
Nathaniel Lyon	Brigadier General[45]

When former President Grant visited California in 1879 at the conclusion of his world tour General Vallejo's wife, and daughter Luisa attended the welcoming ceremonies in San Francisco. Luisa described those ceremonies to her ailing father who remained at home. On September 27, 1879, the old, original Californio acknowledged his daughter's note:

> I just received your letter. Tell Mamma that pleases me that you all have had such a good time. The picture that the newspapers have printed about the ovation given to General Grant; that of Oakland must have been more impressive to the American Chief.[46]

This, then, is all we know about any possible connection between the young Grant and the distinguished first citizen of California, General M. G. Vallejo.

At the close of his Benicia duty, Grant faced an official hearing which has created a measure of misunderstanding to this day. On Saturday, September 4, 1852, a Board of Survey was convened, "to investigate and report upon the losses and damages of public property" which occurred in Panama under Grant's charge as the regimental quartermaster. Such a board was the normal military administrative device to determine liability of

[45] Robert D. Parmelee, *Pioneer Sonoma* (Sonoma, Calif., 1972) p. 84.
[46] Madie Brown Emparan, *The Vallejos of California* (San Francisco, 1968), p. 408.

government property loss. About $1,350 worth of the 4th Infantry clothing and garrison equipment was lost or destroyed during the unpleasant crossing.

Grant, in the terse, straightforward writing style which became his trademark, officially reported on that loss. He described the failure of the contractor to carry the baggage across the Isthmus and his efforts to find alternative transportation. Grant told of the cholera outbreak, hiring the natives to replace sick soldiers, and of his efforts to get the equipment under cover and under guard.

> But there being a large amount, in bulk and weight, it could not be removed in one day, neither could the natives be kept employed at night. — Hence a portion of the property was left one night unprotected.
>
> Had transportation been furnished promptly at Cruces, as it should have been under the contract, it is my opinion that but little or no loss would have been sustained.

The Board found no fault with Grant. The Board "concluded that every exertion was used by officers to protect public property from loss or damage."[47]

Actually Grant spent little time at Benicia Barracks. With the 4th Infantry, he was assigned there in August and September 1852, when he first arrived in California to recuperate from the arduous Isthmus of Panama crossing. He was officially posted there for temporary duty as a member of a court-martial panel in May and June 1853, but since the court-martial was called off at the last minute, he spent little (or no) time in Benicia. In June 1854 he passed by Benicia on his way to and from Knight's Ferry after he resigned from the army and just prior to returning home to Missouri.

---

[47]Grant, *Papers*, pp. 261-62.

In recent years a Benicia Chamber of Commerce promotional folder continued to report: "Still standing on the arsenal property... is the guardhouse where young Ulysses S. Grant is said to have once been confined."[48] This was the "trial" reported on the historical sign posted in front of the guard house. These inaccurate citations refer to the routine Board of Survey inquiry, not a trial and not requiring confinement. But in a sense these notes, issued in good faith, emphasize the almost tragic reporting that has clouded the service of Grant in the West. Grant's alleged reputation as a drinking man who was practically drummed out of the army started on the Pacific Coast and stuck to him to the end of his days.

---

[48] William H. Jacob letter to the author, May 4, 1976.

Chapter IV

To and From Columbia Barracks

The 4th Infantry left Benicia September 14, 1852, in the *Columbia* bound for Oregon Territory. The regiment was ordered to spread its force over Northern California and Oregon to establish posts and protect the settlers. Grant called the ship "a nice little steamer that is perfectly sea-worthy." As it turned out, seaworthy she was, but seasick proof, she was not.[1]

The newly-built *Columbia* arrived on the Pacific Coast in October 1850. Originally intended for the mail service between San Francisco and Oregon, she was used occasionally on the Panama run between 1851 and 1854. The medium-sized steamer was about one-third the size of the *Golden Gate,* and had three decks and three masts. On the main deck *Columbia* had a 70-foot dining saloon with staterooms on each side. The lower cabins aft and forward could accommodate 150 passengers.[2]

The whole company, including Grant and some of the *Columbia's* officers became seasick on the voyage. Grant

---

[1] Grant, *Papers*, p. 262.
[2] Kemble, *op. cit.*, p. 220.

reported that the "trip from San Francisco [was] the roughest that I have ever experienced... The wind blew for three days most terrifically..."[3]

Grant looked forward to duty at Columbia Barracks and hoped "that I will be as much pleased with Van Couver as I am with... Calafornia."[4] Five days after leaving San Francisco he saw Astoria, Oregon, a town, he said, of about thirty homes clinging to the side of a hill covered with tall trees. Grant noted to Julia that he had seen Astoria on maps and read about it, but it wasn't much, except for its location at the mouth of the Columbia with custom house and post office. It had no visible means of economic support, not even a wharf.[5] Here John Jacob Astor had tried to build a fort and a fur trading post to control commerce in the Pacific Northwest, but he lost it when his isolated lieutenants sold it to the British during the War of 1812.

In anticipation Grant wrote:

> I have no doubt but I shall like Oregon very much. Evry one speaks well of the climate and the growing prospects of the country. It has timber and agricultural land, and the best market in the world for all they can produce. Evry article of produce can be raised here than can be in the states; and with much less labor, and finds a ready cash market at four times the value the same article would bring at home.[6]

By 9 p.m., Sunday evening September 19, the *Columbia* was moving up the broad river and her passengers expected to be at Columbia Barracks by breakfast the next morning.

---

[3] Grant, *Papers*, p. 265.

[4] *Ibid.*, p. 263.

[5] *Ibid.*, p. 265.

[6] *Ibid.*, p. 266.

Fort Vancouver was located on the north bank of the Columbia River in what is now southern Washington, about six miles from Portland. For a quarter of a century the Fort had served as headquarters and main depot of the Hudson's Bay Company operations west of the Rocky Mountains. The stockaded, fur-trading post was the economic, political, and social hub of the Pacific Northwest.

In 1824 the Hudson's Bay Company decided to move its western headquarters from Fort George, at the mouth of the Columbia River, to the Vancouver site 124 miles above. The next year a new fort was built close to the river, surrounded by cultivated fields. It grew rapidly in size and importance. The Hudson's Bay Company had a virtual monopoly of the fur trade in "Oregon Country" which then included present-day Oregon and Washington, and other territory, as well as the coast that supplied seal and sea otter skins. The firm's huge Columbia Department stretched from the Rockies to the Pacific, from Russian Alaska to Mexican California, with outposts on San Francisco Bay and in Hawaii. Fort Vancouver was the nerve center of this vast commercial empire. Much of the cultural life of the Oregon Country revolved about Vancouver. Here was established the first school, the first circulating library, the first theater, and several of the earliest churches in the Pacific Northwest.

As American settlers began to flow into the Oregon Country, heading for the Willamette Valley, British-owned Fort Vancouver was a major stopping point. Here were the only adequate supplies of food, seed, and farm implements in the Northwest.

The treaty of 1846 between the United States and Great Britain established the 49th parallel, just above

Puget Sound, as the southern boundary of Canada. It was a compromise between British desire for everything north of the Columbia River and the American goal expressed by "Fifty-four Forty or Fight." The treaty put Fort Vancouver squarely in American territory, and the influence of the post and the Hudson's Bay continued to decline. American settlers began to squat on land near Fort Vancouver. To protect itself the company welcomed the establishment of a U. S. Army camp in 1849. A military reservation was created around the old fur trading post and slowly the English were eased out.[7]

At the height of its prosperity Fort Vancouver was an imposing establishment; the log stockade enclosure measured 734 feet by 318 feet. A tower at the northwest corner housed eight cannon, fired to salute company ships in port. Their presence also discouraged attacks upon the Fort by American settlers during the boundary dispute.

Outside the stockade, houses, barns, and workshops sprawled over the company's landholdings. Only about thirty people lived inside the Fort but more than 300

[7]Selected, general historical sources were consulted for the preparation of this chapter. Citations for the sources are in the bibliography or specifically cited in these chapter notes. Most helpful were: Ted Van Arsdol, "Vancouver Barracks," *Clark County History*, 1966, and Milton Bona, "U.S. Grant at Vancouver," *Clark County History*, 1974. Also, John A. Hussey, *The History of Fort Vancouver and Its Physical Structure;* Washington State Historical Society; *Fort Vancouver*, leaflet published by The National Parks Service; Carl Landerholm, "Cayuse to Cadillac, Clark County Washington History told by Contemporaries;" Robert and Louise Clark, "historical papers," prepared for Fort Vancouver National Historical Site; Robert W. Frazer, *Forts of the West;* M. Leona Nicols, "Captain Grant and his Poor Potato Patch," *Sunday Oregonian*, Feb. 26, 1939; *The Official History of The Washington National Guard*, Vol. 1, "Heritage of the Washington Territorial Militia;" Erma Fordyce Clark, "History of Vancouver Barracks," compiled from notes made on records stored in the vault at Post Headquarters, undated; and Herbert M. Hart, *Old Forts of the Northwest*.

Ground Plan of Fort Vancouver Military Reservation, 1854.
Drawn by Joseph K. Mansfield, it shows Lt. Col. Bonneville's
headquarters (now called "the Grant House") where the letter
"A" is circled. The "Quartermaster's Ranch" where Grant
lived is where the letter "B" is circled.

Gustave Sohon's drawing of Fort Vancouver, 1854.
The original is in the U.S. Archives, Washington, D.C.

were close by in an area that came to be known as Kanaka (Hawaiian) Village, a neat cluster of three dozen or so dwellings built along rough streets or lanes. Other houses were scattered widely over the floodplain. A company wharf was built on the riverbank next to the company's storehouse and boatsheds.[8]

Companies L and M of the First Artillery commanded by Brevet Major J. S. Hatheway arrived on the Columbia River in May 1849. The army established a tent camp on the well-cleared space on the slope above the Hudson's Bay stockade, leased a few buildings, and called the post Columbia Barracks. When Capt. Rufus Ingalls, assistant quartermaster of the Pacific Division, arrived he erected several permanent structures to serve as winter quarters. "The Grant House," now a museum, was one of those. It is a large two-story, originally built of logs, with siding added in the 1870s. Ulysses Grant did not live in "The Grant House," but actually resided at a handsome house nearer the river. He did, however, frequent "The Grant House" since it was regimental headquarters.

Columbia Barracks, with its carefully laid out officer's row and parade grounds, overlooked the river about a mile up a gentle slope. It was truly an inspired location for an army post. Spruce and fir were everywhere, Mount Hood was awesome in the distance with its snow cap much of the year, and the broad Columbia was as pretty as any river in America.

Columbia Barracks was designated Fort Vancouver in July 1853. Vancouver Arsenal was established in connection with the post in 1859, and the name was changed to Vancouver Barracks in April 1879. Hudson's Bay Company hung on until 1860 when they moved their

---

[8]National Park Service, "Fort Vancouver National Historical Site," U. S. Dept. of the Interior, Wash., D.C., 1981.

depleted stores to Vancouver Island, British Columbia; as they departed, they turned over the keys to the small army contingeht. By 1871 the United States had paid Great Britain $650,000 in settlement of the Hudson's Bay Company claim for the value of Fort Vancouver.

The Indians on the lower Columbia lived in small, family villages. They had no reason to move around like their brethren on the plains because everything they needed was close at hand — salmon, game, and native foods such as camas, wapato and acorns. When they did wish to travel they used their dugout canoes on streams and lakes. These Indians were peaceful, living without territorial disputes; only when one family group tried to enslave another did fighting break out. The Indians were important to the economy of the region because they collected furs and exchanged them with Hudson's Bay Company, and other traders, for items they wanted; blankets, tobacco, trinkets, and guns.

After his arrival Grant filed a report with the Pacific Division's Chief Quartermaster commenting on Indian affairs. He pointed out that there were a few Clickitats in the vicinity of Columbia Barracks and an occasional Cowlitz or Dalles tribal member passed through. Capt. Grant wrote that all of these Indians were "easily controlled and altogether too insignificant in prowess & numbers to need much care or attention, and even this poor remnant of a once powerful tribe is fast wasting away before those blessings of civilization whisky and Small pox."[9]

Grant was impressed with the Hudson's Bay Company overall treatment of the Indians. He saw the Company paying for Indian labor, teaching them how to

[9]Grant, *Papers,* p. 310.

farm and to herd, and charging fair prices for good merchandise. During his stint on the Columbia, Grant saw the Indians dying "off very fast... acquiring the vices of the white people... [and] also their diseases. The measles and the small-pox were both amazingly fatal." Years later he remembered the good Company doctor who established a hospital for the Indians close by Grant's residence. Nearly every case he treated recovered, Grant recalled.[10]

The army's visiting inspector wrote in his 1854 report: "There are no Indians near [Fort Vancouver] of consequence in a military point of view... there is nothing here to be feared from their warriors.[11]

The troops that landed with U. S. Grant at Columbia Barracks on September 20, 1852, numbered almost 300. By November 1853, their numbers were down to 118 because of dispersals throughout the Pacific Northwest.[12] In spite of his keen interest and excitement with the new surroundings, Grant was feeling low and blue. He had received no letter from Julia except one written before she knew the regiment had departed from Governors Island — more than two months and thousands of dangerous miles past.

By early fall Capt. Grant had settled into Columbia Barracks routine. He liked Oregon Territory even though it was frightfully expensive. He was particularly pleased to report to Julia that he had made $1,500 in a partnership with the Headquarter's sutler, Elijah E. Camp, and expected to make more than $5,000 in his first year. Grant's financial rollercoaster, up and down, had

---

[10]Grant, *Memoirs*, p. 206.

[11]Robert W. Frazer, ed., *Mansfield on the Condition of the Western Forts* (Norman, 1963).

[12]Grant, *Papers*, p. 269.

begun. It turned out that the partnership with Camp made only paper profits, never realizing a true gain. On October 7, his spirits were so high he even dared to hope that Julia and the children would be joining him early in the coming year.[13]

Before the end of October, 1852, Grant had taken a river steamer up to the army's post at The Dalles where he spent a week. Fort Dalles, ninety miles up the Columbia, had been established several years earlier to be of assistance to the large number of settlers who were streaming into Oregon on the overland route. One company of 69 men, under the command of Brevet Major Alvord, was posted there.[14]

During the latter half of the 1850s Fort Dalles became an important army center. Its geographical location made it key to the first "road" through Oregon for several years. The Dalles, considered by many to be the end of the Oregon Trail, was a natural landing place where the bluffs of the Columbia Gorge widened out. It was the last rest stop before the final obstacle facing the westbound immigrants — the Cascade Mountains.[15]

Enthusiastic investor that he had become, Grant purchased cattle and hogs at The Dalles for "speculation," and a handsome and spirited horse for himself. He rode his horse back to Vancouver down the small bridle trail along the south side of the river.

Through no particular fault of the principals involved, a conflict of authority arose between Grant, regimental quartermaster, and Capt. Thomas Lee Brent of Virginia, post quartermaster. Perhaps a commander more skillful

[13]*Ibid.*, p. 268.

[14]Lewis, *Sheffield*, p. 57.

[15]Priscilla Knuth, "Picturesque Frontier: The Army's Fort Dalles." Reprinted from the *Oreg. Hist. Qtly.*, Dec. 1966.

than Lt. Col. Bonneville would have solved the problem but disagreement continued for seven months until Brent eventually was transferred. The arrangements that were made left Ulysses Grant free to concentrate on outfitting survey parties. When Brent departed, Grant took over his assignments as well.[16]

Between October and December, 1852, Capt. Grant kept busy with his duties and attempted to add to his capital. Grant lived with Ingalls, Brent, and three clerks at "Quartermaster's Ranch." This imposing house was prefabricated in New England and shipped in sections around Cape Horn to become the first permanent building at Vancouver. It was located about 400 yards west of the stockade, near the river and was the best building on the post. Grant considered it the finest home in Oregon Territory, and it probably was. The attractive building had high ceilings, a broad porch on three sides, two stories, and it stood apart from other army structures. Lt. Col. Bonneville had to put up with a log house that had rough floors and chinked cracks while the quartermaster's house became Columbia Barracks social center.[17]

Rufus Ingalls and Sam Grant had not seen each other for seven years. Friends since they roomed together at West Point, they became even closer companions at Vancouver. They took long horseback rides together, remembered their school days, played cards, and entertained visiting survey officers in the evenings. Ingalls and Grant became known as the post's most notable characters and their card games, for small stakes, became

[16]Grant, *Papers*, pp. 271-74.

[17]Milton Bona, "The Truth About U. S. Grant at Vancouver," *Clark County History*, 1974, pp. 428 and 431. It is understandable that even the authorative Grant, *Papers* confuse Vancouver's museum "Grant House" with the quartermaster's house. *See* Grant, *Papers*, p. 282.

legendary.[18] Rufe, years later, told how Sam "astonished his brother officers by his clear, luminous descriptions" of the fighting in Mexico. Others were impressed with Grant's memory of small battle incidents and his thoughtful critiques of his commander's strategy and tactics. Quartermaster's Ranch was a lively place during the rainy evenings of fall and winter and a genial atmosphere prevailed.[19]

It appeared that Columbia Barracks was positioned properly to become a permanent post and that the Fourth Infantry might be stationed there for years. Grant was convinced that he must settle down, make some money, and bring his family out to this pleasant environment.

When Capts. Grant, Ingalls and Wallen heard that ice was selling for outrageous prices in San Francisco, they cut and loaded 100 tons aboard a sailing schooner, including the Captain as a partner. After several months the Captain returned with no money, but a sad story. Winds were against him, the ice melted and other ice ships from Alaska grabbed the business. The officers lost their investment.[20]

Grant rounded up cattle and pigs for shipment to San Francisco where Wallen was to sell them. "We continued that business until both of us lost all the money we had," recalled Wallen, but when he returned to Vancouver, Wallen owed Grant three or four hundred dollars which he could not pay until later. Another disappointment.[21]

Grant was forced to take several week's sick leave in

---

[18]Frank A. Burr, *General U. S. Grant* (Boston, 1885), p. 117.

[19]Lloyd Lewis, *Captain Sam Grant* (Boston, 1950), pp. 310-11. Grant's friend Ingalls was at Appomattox Courthouse that fateful day in 1865. It was to his friend that Grant turned to relieve the tension when a deeply-saddened Robert E. Lee departed.

[20]*Ibid.*, p. 312.

[21]Burr, *op. cit.*, p. 116.

early December to recover from a nasty cold that would not give up and brought on severe cramps. "I have suffered so much that I walk like an old man of eighty," he wrote.[22] Capt. Grant did not recover quickly and was forced to spend time indoors on toast and tea. He wrote Julia that he had suffered terribly from cramps in his legs and in one hand. If he could just keep dry, Grant wrote to his wife, he could get back on his feet. It was the rainy season and he was continually wet and cold,[23] but, he was well cared for by Private Getz and his wife Margaret. Maggy had been the Grant's servant at a previous post and her efficiency and loyalty to Grant made him "envied by evry body that comes to the house."[24] The Getzs were like members of Grant's family and there was much mutual respect between them.

He leased a tract of land from Mr. W. Nye about a mile from the post. With Capts. Wallen, Brent and McConnell, about one hundred acres was cleared and fenced in order to plant potatoes and oats. Grant purchased two sickly horses that had worked their way across the plains the previous summer. Under his expert care they recuperated rapidly and became a good team for ploughing the farm. With his horses Capt. Sam broke the ground while his partners did the planting.[25]

Ulysses continued to send financial reports to Julia. "[If] I collect all that is due me . . . there is about eighteen hundred dollars." He did admit that one officer "had sacrificed his word" on a two hundred dollar loan. Grant had failed to obtain written confirmation of the advance and the debtor had disappeared in San Francisco.[26]

Grant labored on his farm and noted that for those

---

[22]Grant, *Papers*, p. 275. [23]*Ibid.*, p. 277. [24]*Ibid.*, p. 276.
[25]Grant, *Memoirs*, p. 203. [26]Grant, *Papers*, p. 275.

willing to work hard Oregon was the best "place I have ever seen."

> Timber stands close to the banks of the river free for all. Wood is worth five dollars per cord for steamers. The soil produces almost double any place I have been before with the finest market in the world for it after it is raised... beef gets fat without feeding... [and] chickens [sell for] one dollar each...[27]

As the eventful year of 1852 drew to a close, Ulysses realized that Julia and the boys could not join him. For the first time he concluded that he would prefer to get out of the army than continue the separation. Grant's best hope for seeing his family lay in obtaining his long-anticipated promotion and receiving orders for Washington D.C. to straighten out old accounts. Already he loved the West: if Julia, Fred and Ulysses Jr. were with him on the Pacific Coast, he wrote his wife, "I wouldn't care to ever go back."[28]

As 1853 began the young Captain was grossly agitated with the mails. He could not accept delays of two months for each letter. He missed Julia terribly and was increasingly heartsick with longings to see his little boys. Grant's mood became as blustery as the weather. "It either rains or snows here all the time," he wrote on January 3rd, "so I scarsely ever get a mile from home, and half the time do not go out of the house during the day." He was feeling better physically, however, and reassured his wife that he was well and was heavier then ever before. Grant even reported a minor adventure when he and Ingalls were the first of that season to walk over the frozen Columbia river.[29]

---

[27] *Ibid.*, p. 278.
[28] *Ibid.*
[29] *Ibid.*, p. 279.

As the weather moderated Ulysses's spirits rose. He hoped to finish ploughing his farm soon, he believed Columbia Barracks to be the best station in Oregon, and thought that when he was promoted to a company commander he could return to the East and bring his family back with him to the Pacific Coast. Grant wanted to command a company at Vancouver but he suspected that he might have to go to a more primitive post.

Grant wrote Julia further financial details in mid-February. He did not wish to send any money home at that time because he needed every dollar for seed to plant potatoes, oats and vegetables on his farm. He was upset that Camp, who owed him $1,500, was living prosperously and giving no sign of beginning payments on his note.[30]

By March 4, Ulysses was tired and sore from his manual labor on the farm but almost all of the planting was in, and he and his partners were looking forward to a future pay off. But he was pressed for cash: even though others owed him over $2,000, the obligations did not become due for six to eight months. Grant saw financial hard times until the fall of 1853.

Capt. Brent's transfer meant more commissary routine for Grant, and he was worried about how to balance his professional and his outside interests and still earn the potential income he needed so desperately. But he believed that Brent might return East to pick up his family and Julia could return West with the Brents. Ulysses still hoped that the long separation might be ended, but he was concerned that his promotion might take him from Vancouver, a good family post.[31]

---

[30]*Ibid.*, p. 289.
[31]*Ibid.*, pp. 291-92.

If there was any prospect of my being promoted to one of the companies [here]. . . I would be delighted to have you here. There is not a more delightful place in the whole country . . . [32]

As spring approached Grant continued his physical work in the fields. He found that he could do all the ploughing and furrowing himself and was surprised that he could do it so well. "I never worked before with so much pleasure," he wrote his wife, "because now I feel sure that evry day will bring a large reward." Also he found time to manage a wood cut operation with his own horses and wagon, and prepared to enter the general draying business. He believed that by fall he would reap substantial profits from his ventures, promising never again to get into debt. Ulysses was worried that his impending promotion might send him to Humboldt Bay where no family quarters existed. [33]

Capt. Grant started growing a beard when he left California. In his first letter home headed "Washington Territory" (Congress had divided the Oregon territory in March 1853), he reported that his beard was several inches long. [34] Except for short periods later in his life, the beard stayed and changed Grant's appearance dramatically.

Between May 15 and June 14, 1853, Ulysses was away from Columbia Barracks. He was ordered to Benicia to testify in a court-martial that was cancelled at the last minute when the accused officer resigned. Grant checked in with his friends in San Francisco; the Stevens, the Gladwins and young Mr. Dodge, all formerly of Sackets Harbor. Also, he visited Knight's Ferry for another

[32] Ibid., p. 294.
[33] Ibid., pp. 294-95.
[34] Ibid., p. 298

pleasant week with the Dent brothers. From San Francisco he expressed again his loneliness to his beloved Julia:

> My dear wife it is very hard to be seperated from you so long but until I am better off it cannot be helped. If I can get together a few thousand dollars I shall most certainly go home...[35]

While in San Francisco he made some arrangements "to do a conciderable business, in a commission way."[36] One large firm, from which he purchased flour and other army supplies, asked Grant to report on commodity prices in the territories. Prices were so unstable that the San Francisco merchant believed early notification would allow him to ship articles that would reap sizable profits. The company would furnish the merchandise, Grant would sell it, and the profits would be divided. Also, while in San Francisco, Grant and a partner purchased barrels of pork for delivery to Vancouver. They were priced higher up north and the enterprising young Captain was confident of clearing about six hundred dollars.[37]

With several other officers including Capt. Wallen and Thomas H. Stevens, Grant took out a one year lease for some space in the old Union Hotel in San Francisco for five hundred dollars a month. They planned to convert the area into a private billiard room and club, and sell memberships. There were so many unattached males around that the idea appeared feasible. But, alas, the hired manager departed with the officer's funds so the venture failed.[38]

[35] Ibid., p. 300.

[36] Ibid., p. 301.

[37] Ibid., p. 304.

[38] Historical Magazine, Sept. 1867, 2nd Series, Vol. II. p. 179, and Bruce Catton, U. S. Grant and the American Military Tradition (New York, 1954), p. 49.

When Grant returned to Columbia Barracks, he found that disaster had struck. The unpredictable river had wiped out his hard labor and his hopes for a good return on his farming efforts. All of his grain, onions, corn and most of the enormous potato crop was ruined. His wood business was in disarray because of the flooding. He caught another severe cold, but had to keep busy outfitting survey parties directed by the new territorial governor Major Isaac Stevens and including Capt. George B. McClellan as one leader.[39] Because of these duties, Grant had no time to dwell on his severe financial loss. He did think about resigning from the army but promised Julia to "weight the matter well before I act."[40]

Capt. Grant occasionally crossed the Columbia to ride down to Portland or Oregon City on the Willamette River. Oregon City was larger than its neighboring village and was the trading and cultural center of that area. Grant, sometimes accompanied by one of his fellow officers, enjoyed the ride and the change of scenery. The Hudson's Bay Company former chief factor, 6 foot 4 inch Dr. John McLoughlin, the "Father of Oregon," had chosen picturesque Oregon City as a place to retire.

Grant was surprised one day in Portland when the sheriff of nearby Washington County attached his army mount just as Capt. Sam got off the boat from Vancouver. Adams & Co., a large, territorial wholesaler, through their agent Richard E. Wiley, had filed suit in the District Court against Quartermaster Grant for $1,200. Grant accompanied the sheriff to see Wiley, where arrangements were made to satisfy the debt, which was official

---

[39]Grant, *Papers*, pp. 301-03.
[40]*Ibid.*, p. 301.

army business. Court records note that the suit was dropped in August 1853.

The Hillsboro, Oregon, newspaper recounted the story in 1900:

U. S. Grant Sued Here
Default and Judgment for $1200 Were Taken

The Famous Soldier's Horse Was Seized
But He Paid the Debt and Went His Way

...Strange as it may appear the case was overlooked by the papers of that day and the fact that a man who was afterward elected President was once sued in an Oregon court has never before been made history...[41]

In late June 1853, Grant, spirits up and optimism soaring, wrote Julia that "Evry thing that I have undertaken, as a speculation, has proved profitable. I have though been unfortunate in some respects... the result of high waters!" He explained that the portion of his potato crop that survived should bring high prices because of the shortage.[42] But again he was disappointed: the only potatoes sold were to Grant's own mess.[43] Grant reported to his wife:

I have spoken of speculations so much that the subject is becoming painful... I told you... of all the *downs* of all I have done. (Before I had never met with a *down*.) Since that I have made several hundreds in speculations of various sorts. In groceries which I do not sell, and which are not retailed. I have now a large quantity of pork on hand which is worth to-day ten dollar pr. barrel more than I gave for it...[44]

[41]Court docket notation Grant, *Papers*, p. 416. Newspaper clipping from Hillsboro, Oreg., Aug. 15, 1900. Oreg. Hist. Soc. Portland, Oreg. Scrapbook 35, page 112,
[42]Grant, *Papers*, p. 304.
[43]Grant, *Memoirs*, p. 203.
[44]Grant, *Papers*, p. 306.

After the potato disaster, Grant hired Sgt. Sheffield to buy up all the chickens within twenty miles of the post. Capt. Sam and his friend Wallen tried again and chartered a small boat to ship the chickens to San Francisco. Sadly, nearly all the fowl died on the voyage and again the two captains lost their entire investment in that venture.

No one would argue with Capt. Wallen's conclusion:

Neither Grant nor myself had the slightest suggestion of business talent. He was the perfect soul of honor and truth, and believed everyone else as artless as himself.[45]

Grant's debts stayed with him a long time. On June 28, 1855, from Missouri, Ulysses wrote Wallen a promise to pay $300 resulting from "our unfortunate San Francisco speculations." Ten years later, on December 29, 1865, Lt. General Grant sent Wallen a check cancelling the debt.[46] Thus did Grant live with his obligations in contrast to the many who forgot their debts to him.

With all of his financial troubles and his loneliness, it should be noted that Grant's experiences at Vancouver were not all adverse. He was among friends he enjoyed, and in a location that was, except for occasionally excessive rainfall, delightful. And, after all, he and his companions were high spirited young soldiers away from the normal restraints of civilization.

Primitive though the area was, a little theater blossomed. Drum Major Elderkin recalled that there was "excellent dramatic talent" available, and that he and his wife Mary were active members of the troop that played a number of Shakespearean pieces and others, including "Golden Farmer, Jemmy Twitcher in England!" On

---

[45]Burr, op. cit., 116.

[46]Page 21 of an unidentified catalog announcing sale of historical letters: Grant items were "Two Autograph Letters Signed," no. 181. Ulysses S. Grant Assoc., Carbondale, Ill.

THEATRE.

VANCOUVER THESPIAN CORPS

On next TUESDAY Evening, September 6th, 1853,

Will be presented (for the 2nd time,) the DRAMA in [...] (received with great applause on its last presentation) of

GOLDENFARMER,

Jemmy Twitcher in England !

Golden Farmer,	Lieas.	Jemmy Twitcher.	Smith.
Harry Hammer,	Caldwell.	Old Mobb,	Fox.
William Harvey,	Stanton.	Lord Fitzallen,	Wright.
John,	Rodgers,	Thomas,	Sheridan.
1st. Officer,	Comstock,	2nd. Officer,	Orr.
Elizabeth,	Mrs Kelly	Mrs Kelly.	Miss E. Kelly.
Jenny.	Villagers, Servants &c.	JK. Hammer,	Orr.

After which, SONG, - - "You'll remember me," - Stanton.

The Evening's entertainment to conclude with the Favorite Vaudeville—in one act—of

THE LOAN OF A LOVER,

Peter Spyke,	Wright	Ino,	Lang.
Swyzel,	Fox,	Pd,	Md. Wright.
Captain Amersfort.	Stanton.	anna Beauregard.	Mrs. Fox.

☞ The DRAMA (in three Acts) of "ST. PATRICK'S EVE, or the Order of the Day" Is In rehearsal, and will shortly be produced.

Doors open at Half-past Seven, the performance to commence at Half-past eight o'clock.

Box $1.   Parquette 50c.

A Handbill from the Vancouver Thespians, 1853.
Cited in *Oregon Imprints: 1845-1870,* by George Belknap.

Grant House Museum as it appears today.
The structure was erected in 1849.
Courtesy, Clark County Historical Museum.

September 6, 1853, Grant probably attended the performance. The Vancouver Thespian Corps produced this drama for a second time, its promoters claiming that it had received "great applause on its initial performance." Doors opened at half-past seven, and the performance began at half-past eight o'clock. It cost 50¢ a ticket; one dollar for a box seat.[47]

It could have been this evening that Delia Sheffield described when she wrote:

> On one occasion we were having some private theatricals, in our little theater at the post, when a drunken man... was disturbing the audience, Captain Grant walked to where he was sitting, and taking him firmly by the collar, marched him out of the hall. He had a true soldier's love of order.[48]

Other incidents brightened the days. Lt. Col. Bonneville had reveille sounded at 5 a.m. every morning. Capt. McConnell, as adjutant, was required to be present although he thought it was a waste of good sleeping time. Usually, the adjutant stayed as far away from his commander as possible, stationing himself about fifty yards behind the colonel and always appearing "very pouty." One morning, during a lull in the ceremony, the colonel said to his adjutant:

"A penny for your thoughts, Mr. McConnell."

"I was just wondering," the adjutant said, "whether I should ever get so old that I couldn't sleep in the morning."

T. M. Anderson, later the commander at the post, wrote that within the hour Bonneville had appointed a new adjutant.[49]

---

[47] Ruth F. Erickson, "Old Slocum House — 1966," *Clark County History*, 1966. The 1853 handbill is on page 146 of her article.

[48] Lewis, *Sheffield*, p. 61.

[49] Ted Van Arsdol, "Vancouver Barracks," previously cited, p. 99.

On some evenings, quartermaster's ranch would ring with the cheerful sounds of partying. The dining room was cleared for dancing, and the regimental band would play until past midnight. Guests arrived from Astoria and Portland; even the Governor's daughter travelled from Oregon City. According to one partygoer Capt. Grant would never take part in the dancing, but would come in and look on for awhile and then retreat upstairs to his room where he remained all evening smoking.[50] It would be easy to believe that his thoughts were centered upon Julia and how much he missed her, especially in the festivities of simple society.

In September 1853, Capt. Grant wrote pleas, almost desperate ones, to the army's quartermaster general and the army's commissary general, both in Washington D.C., asking for orders to return to the nation's capital to settle troublesome accounts left over from the Mexican War. Although Lt. Col. Bonneville endorsed the request, the quartermaster general replied in December, "There is no necessity for your presence at Washington to settle your accounts;" the Subsistence Department answered in kind; "no necessity exists for your presence..."[51] Thus, Grant's last hope of being ordered East, which would allow him to join his family, was turned down by the army without serious consideration.

Unknown to him, Grant's promotion to full Captain in the regular army was effective on August 9, 1853. Secretary of War Jefferson Davis ordered him to "proceed, without delay, to join your company (F.) at Fort Humboldt, California."[52] Now Ulysses's worst fears

---

[50]Lewis, *Sheffield*, p. 60.

[51]Grant, *Papers*, pp. 311-13.

[52]*Ibid.*, p. 312. The formal commission was not signed by President Franklin Pierce until Feb. 9, 1854, and Grant was not notified until two months later.

were about to be realized. Fort Humboldt had no family quarters, was remote, and commanded by an officer who did not like Grant.

Eureka, California, 1854.
Artist Juan Buckingham Wandesford was commissioned by Eureka's first mayor, James Talbot Ryan, to paint this picture. The Ryan & Duff mill is on the right. The original painting was given to the City of Eureka by Ryan's granddaughter and now hangs in the Mayor's office.
Courtesy of Lynwood Carranco

Chapter V

"How Forsaken
I Feel Here"

On January 5, 1854, Captain Grant reported to Fort Humboldt. His transfer there set in motion a series of events that temporarily sped his personal deterioration, his drinking so misunderstood by later critics, and his resignation from the army that had been his life.[1]

"Splendid" Humboldt Bay was discovered by Boston-born Captain Jonathan Winship in 1806 while hunting sea otter for his employer, the Russian-American Fur Company. In spite of being perhaps the best harbor between San Francisco and the mouth of the Columbia, a series of famed explorers from Cabrillo and Drake to Vancouver sailed the coast without detecting it. Winship's men luckily spotted the hidden entrance and he recorded the discovery. Dr. Josiah Gregg's party rediscovered the bay in late 1849 as they came over the mountains from interior California and down the coast seeking the mouth of the Trinity River. Gold had been discovered at the headwaters of the Trinity that year, and

---

[1] The title of Chapter 5 comes from U. S. Grant's Feb. 2, 1854, letter to Julia Dent Grant from Fort Humboldt, Calif. Grant wrote of his growing loneliness and despondency from having no word from Julia since Oct. 1853.

prospecting parties were exploring between the Trinity, the Klamath, and the coast. As rich diggings were found, the need to support them by coastal settlements became apparent.[2]

A brief review of the founding of the bay communities will help to describe the society into which Grant settled in 1854.

In April of 1850, the schooner *Laura Virginia* anchored in the bay. The leaders of the "Association" formed in San Francisco to colonize the area called it Humboldt, and off-loaded settlers. The first village, named Humboldt City, was founded opposite the harbor's difficult entrance but proved to be ill-sited for traffic to the Klamath mines and by September 1851, had stopped growing.

Union Town (now Arcata), on a beautiful plateau at the northern end of the bay, became the county seat when Humboldt County was organized in 1853. It was the coastal terminal of the pack trains that carried supplies from ships to the miners on the Klamath and Trinity rivers. Union was surrounded by excellent farm and timber lands, but never was a decent port because of hazardous mud flats close in to shore.

Lumbering later replaced mining as the chief activity of the area. Eureka, the last town to be settled on the bay, was located on deep water and was the natural shipping point for the area. As the Klamath mines were exhausted and the Trinity mining district became more important, Eureka was not at a locational disadvantage and began its ascendency. Only seven miles from the bay's entrance, it was the true head of navigation. Since 1856, when it

---

[2]Owen Cochran Coy, *The Humboldt Bay Region, 1850-1875* (Los Angeles, 1929), p. xi.

became the county seat, Eureka has been the leading town in the area and later the largest lumber shipping port on the West Coast.

Bucksport, on the bay and a few miles southwest of Eureka, was surveyed and, since it was on the main channel of the bay near its entrance, settlers were attracted to it.[3] The establishment of Fort Humboldt on the bluff overlooking Bucksport gave the community an added boost in 1853, but the town never prospered and, indeed, it was only the presence of the Fort that kept it alive. Today Bucksport is a memory at the southern boundary of Eureka.

As the Humboldt Bay settlements grew so did the "Indian problem." The Indians had walked the forests, fished the rivers, and hunted the plentiful game for centuries. They had villages and hunting grounds hard by the bay and were not interested in moving on as the pressing white settlers expected them to do. The small bands of Indians that lived on the bay "were poor, harmless... and miserable creatures who lived principally on fish. Many of them were deformed, and the most loathsome looking human beings that I have ever seen," wrote one observer in 1853. "The... Mountain Indians, however, were a different set, and were more or less hostile... [and] killed a good many whites."[4]

In the early 1850s the trouble between the races became more serious and showed no signs of abating. "The packers and miners used little caution in their treatment of the Indians... [shooting them] down when-

[3] Mildred Brooke Hoover, Eugene Hero Rensch, and Ethel Grace Rensch, *Historic Spots in California* (Palo Alto, 1948), p. 245.

[4] Martin F. Schmitt, ed. *General George Crook: His Autobiography* (Norman, 1946), p. 11 (cited hereater as "Crook, *Autobiography*").

ever opportunity offered."[5] The Indians would take revenge indiscriminately and sometimes kill an innocent settler, which in turn might provoke an attack on a nearby Indian rancheria. These continuing frontier hostilities, and increasing pressures from the settlers, led to generally unsettled conditions.[6]

Acting upon urgent requests from Humboldt Bay, and in line with plans to deploy Pacific Department forces where they could operate with maximum effect, Companies "B" and "F" of the 4th Infantry were ordered northward to establish a temporary post. The troops sailed from Benicia on Captain Wright's steamer, *Goliah*, entering the bay on January 30, 1853.[7]

Brevet Lieutenant Colonel Robert C. Buchanan commanded the troops and the following officers: 1st Lt. W. H. Scott, 2nd Lts. Edmund B. Underwood and John C. Bonnycastle, Brevet 2nd Lt. George Crook, and Assistant Surgeon Charles Peter Deyerle. 1st Lt. Lewis Cass Hunt, a first cousin of Eunice Tripler, arrived a few weeks later. Captain Grant would join the garrison the following year.

Robert Christe Buchanan from Maryland had graduated from West Point in 1830. He became an experienced, brave, and well-regarded soldier, but seldom popular with his subordinates. His first combat command was during the "Black Hawk War" in 1832; he fought the Seminoles in Florida; he was in eleven battles and

---

[5]Hoover, *op. cit.*, p. 243.

[6]The early history of Humboldt Bay, the County and coastal towns comes from Coy, *op. cit;* J. M. Guinn, *History of the State of California* (Chicago, 1903); Chad L. Hoopes, *Lure of Humboldt Bay Region* (Dubuque, Iowa);   Hoover, op. cit; and Elliot, cited below.

[7]Coy, *op. cit.*, pp. 141-42.

skirmishes of the Mexican War; and he earned his Brevet Lieutenant Colonelcy in 1847. Buchanan was a senior Captain of Infantry in 1853 and, according to Grant, "expects promotion by evry Mail."[8] He was not named a regular army major, however, until February 3, 1855.

Young George Crook thought that Lt. Col. Buchanan was heartless and cruel. On the sea voyage from Benicia the commander drove the men away from shelter near his cabin door into the rain with the remark that the next thing those soldiers would want would be to dine with their commanding officer in his cabin.

As his acquaintance with Buchanan grew, Crook liked his commanding officer even less. Acting as his adjutant for a short time, Crook was with Buchanan frequently and became familiar with his habits. The young officer attempted to avoid Buchanan whenever possible:

> Our Commander seemed particularly elated at his own importance... and lost no opportunity to impress upon all of us... how far we fell short of what he expected. He seemed to take delight in wounding the feelings of those under him, and succeeded pretty generally in making himself unpopular amongst the citizens as well as the army.[9]

Mary B. Underwood, one month away from giving birth to a son, was the only officer's lady accompanying the group, but there were a few enlisted men's wives. As the little steamer shook and strained crossing the hazardous channel entrance (nearly breaking in two, according to one passenger), the company looked to shore. The impression was decidedly a pleasant one, the beautiful trees, shrubs, and greenery, in contrast to the barren hills

---

[8]Grant, *Papers*, p. 316.
[9]Crook, *Autobiography*, pp. 9-10.

about Benicia.[10] "The sun was shining and everything was lovely. The forest of the immense redwoods which came down close to the bay... presented a beautiful landscape."[11]

Lt. Col. Buchanan spent a few days in reconnaissance and for his new post selected the bluff at Bucksport, about 100 feet above and less than a mile back from the waters of the bay, which today still has an unrivaled view in all directions. The initial military reservation of about 640 acres included open areas to the south, and timber and pasture for grazing to the east. Plenty of fresh water for the new post flowed into a pond south of the bluff and then passed down a narrow marsh between the military reserve and Bucksport into Humboldt Bay.

Among the enthusiastic settlers welcoming the army personnel were the families of James Talbot Ryan and F. S. Duff who lived in frontier style at marshy Eureka. Ryan was Eureka's first citizen and is given credit for being the founding father. Ryan, Duff & Company, using the boiler and engine of a beached steamship, operated the first successful sawmill on the bay.[12] Duff also ran a lodging house and both men furnished supplies for the Fort.

Dr. Jonathan Clark of Bucksport shared his homesite with the Underwoods where, in a tent pitched in his yard, Mrs. Underwood gave birth to a healthy boy, the first child born to the Fort Humboldt family. Mrs. Underwood wrote of those first days:

[10]Wallace W. Elliot, *History of Humboldt County* (San Francisco, 1881), p. 163. "Sketches of Fort Humboldt," by a former resident of the fort, is an excellent summary.

[11]Crook, *Autobiography*, p. 9.

[12]Coy, *op. cit.*, p. 118.

Dr. Clark had a little weatherbeaten office for his home down near the bay below this bluff, with a small kitchen, and tiny cooking stove, and a shed adjoining in which hung the carcass of an elk . . . We arranged with Dr. Clark to live down there and my cook should give him meals for the privilege of using his stove and office as a sitting room when he was away . . . A tent was pitched nearby with a floor, and used for our bedroom. My son was born in that tent the 5th of March 1853.[13]

Reverend A. J. Huestis, who became the first county superintendent of schools in 1855, also was in Bucksport with his family, as were the Maloneys, who kept the small hotel there.

A. P. Marple, a private who arrived in the *Goliah* and was to reside in the region almost 60 years, recalled that the soldiers provided material for framing and finishing the buildings of the Fort by going into the woods and making rough lumber. Marple remembered clearly his aching, tired arms after a day of whip-sawing:

Every officer and soldier had to work in storm or no storm in getting out material . . . a large platform was built for each company to pitch tents on and a large hospital tent was pitched for the sick men.[14]

The two companies pitched their tents to leave a parade ground open in the center, and immediately began building the Fort from the fir and spruce forests which were on two sides of the little plateau. The redwoods

---

[13] Mary B. Underwood to the Postmaster, Eureka, Nov. 4, 1914, published in the *Humboldt Standard*, Nov. 12, 1914. The letter is also in *Susie Baker Fountain Papers*, Vol. 32 (cited hereafter as "Fountain Papers"), pp. 225-27 in the Humboldt State Univ. Lby., Arcata, Calif. Mrs. Underwood's son, E. B. Underwood, Jr., was appointed to the U. S. Naval Academy in 1870 by President U. S. Grant, became Governor of Samoa, and was retired from the Navy as a Commodore in 1911.

[14] A. P. Marple to *West Coast Signal*, Eureka, June 5, 1898. Also in Fountain Papers, *op. cit.*, p. 246. A. P. Marple to *West Coast Signal*, Eureka, Sept 7, 1876. Also in Fountain Papers, *op. cit.*, pp. 211-12.

were so large that logs could not be manhandled. The first structure (later called the Underwood-Simpson house) was well-built, framed, sided with specially fitted logs, weather-boarded and plastered inside. But it took too long to construct, cost too much, and was considered over-built for the climate. The remainder of the buildings were constructed with weather-board and plastered inside.

Game was abundant in the general area. Elk and deer, although plentiful in the mountains close by, seldom were seen in the immediate vicinity of the post. On one occasion, however, the newcomers saw a herd of elk upon the bluff south of the Fort, and bear tracks were seen in the woods adjoining. Most of the post officers enjoyed hunting. The tide flats swarmed with ducks; when they lifted off "the flapping of their wings would sound like distant thunder."[15] Grant noted that "Within eight or ten miles [of the Fort] Deer and occationally Elk and Black Bear are found. Further back [in the mountains] the Grisly Bear are quite numerous."[16]

First Lt. Hunt, as post quartermaster, described Fort Humboldt for official records that first summer of 1853. Hunt thought well of the site, describing the elevated plateau about three miles from the bay's entrance, as a favorable one for supply and for a permanent post should one be needed.

Although he noted that communications were very limited (by sea and by pack trains to the interior), Hunt thought that the surrounding population would increase even though the mountains crowded toward the bay and there was not much room for farming. Hunt thought

[15]Crook, *Autobiography*, p. 11.
[16]Grant, *Papers*, p. 316.

there never would be a large town on the bay. He speculated that wagon roads could not be built and that pack mules would be the major means of land communication for years to come. He remarked about the dangerous entrance and the shifting sandbanks in the channel, but he judged that the harbor was one of the best on the entire Pacific Coast.

Hunt counted "some half dozen saw mills... now in operation" and was impressed with available building materials. At this early date it was evident already that lumbering would be a major economic activity of the area, given the abundance of redwood, Oregon pine, yellow pine, spruce, fir, cottonwood, and red oak in the mountains. Excellent quality bricks were being made in the neighborhood and lime soon would be. The quartermaster noted that local building material prices were set by San Francisco market demand, a fact that would give the growing settlements a problem for years to come.

Hunt reported that the mountain Indians attacked pack trains whenever they had an advantage, but the fearful revenge of the white man against the natives, innocent and guilty alike, made them cautious, especially if the parties moving through the hills seemed on their guard. The army's policy was to send soldiers on the main trails frequently, and Lt. Hunt suggested to San Francisco headquarters that these movements were inexpensive, kept the troops gainfully occupied, pleased the settlers with the appearance of protection, and improved the possibility of understanding between the races.[17]

[17]Lt. Lewis Cass Hunt's observations, many of which have stood the test of time, are in his official report of June 30, 1853, to Major Osborn Cross, Pacific Division Quartermaster at San Francisco. The Natl. Arch., Miscellaneous Records of Dept. of Pacific, Quartermaster files.

Even today Eureka and its sister towns are hemmed in by mountains and remote from the populated centers of the Pacific Coast. Thus, in contrast to most other areas of California, the Humboldt Bay region was unaffected by Spanish and Mexican influences.[18] But mining and timber still created sufficient activity so that Humboldt Bay rivaled San Francisco as the busiest port in California. It is not an exaggeration to characterize Humboldt Bay in 1853 as typical of American western frontier. The area was rough and lonely when Ryan, Duff, Clark, and other pioneers, built the settlements and hosted army personnel

The newly arrived troops, and the few families accompanying them, found Humboldt's climate a bit like San Francisco's, although more inclement, with perhaps twice as many days of rain each year.[19] It was a fairly even climate and, of course, free from the extreme heat and malaria of the Sacramento Valley. But is was usually so cool that a fire inside a dwelling felt good. The drinking water was superb. Army personnel thought Benicia water terrible since it was collected in cisterns during the winter months and stored there for consumption throughout the year. By contrast, Fort Humboldt's water was fresh-tasting and excellent.

Another advantage the new post had over barren and brown Benicia was the abundant growth of beautiful flowers, shrubs, berries of all kinds and, of course, trees. The profusion of blooms which marked the early spring amazed the army families. The variety and beauty of the flowers increased each month until late summer. In back of the post around the pond azaleas flourished, their

[18]Coy, *op. cit.*, p. xi.
[19]Robert J. Roske, *Everyman's Eden; A History of California* (New York, 1968), p. 5.

fragrance floating on the air. California poppies grew in abundance, the best specimens being down by the Eel River.[20] The Indians believed that the golden poppy, which became California's state flower, had special powers.

Pioneer life was not easy. Society was simple and consisted of singing parties at the church, picnic parties on the bay, and an occasional dance. Going to church, reading, visiting with neighbors — sewing for the women, and going to Brett's saloon in Eureka for the men — constituted the social calendar. Shopping was best at Union, but offered few of the opportunities available in San Francisco stores. A major event occurred when a steamer arrived and flags were flown to announce its coming.[21]

The post surgeon, Charles Peter Deyerle, wrote to his family in Virginia between February and August describing the establishment of the Fort and the life he found there in 1853. His observations draw a picture of Humboldt life that is both authoritative and candid:[22]

> We arrived here on the 30th of the month, and after a few days spent in making a reconnaissance of the surrounding country a location was selected on the Bay, near a village called Bucksport, and the troops put in cantonment — there not being a sufficiency of houses in the country to afford us shelter. Since that time we have been engaged in getting out lumber and building houses, which are not yet being completed, we have

[20]Details of the establishment of Fort Humboldt and of the surrounding countryside generally from Elliot, *op. cit.*, Hoopes, *op. cit.*, and the two State of California, Dept. of Parks & Recreation publications on Fort Humboldt, published in 1971 and 1977 and cited in the bibliography. Also *Harriet St. John Simpson Letters*, Appendix A of Chad L. Hoope's unpublished Master's Thesis, Brigham Young Univ., Provo, Utah, 1963 (cited hereafter as "Simpson Letters").

[21]Coy, *op. cit.*, p. 293.

[22]Letters of Charles Peter Deyerle to his family; loaned by his great-great nephew Howard Revercomb Hammond of Greenville, South Carolina.

been and are still living in tents and sheds — though the weather has been quite wet, but not cold.

The Indians are now quiet... They are mostly miserable, degraded class of beings, leading a monastic life, subsisting on roots, seeds, fish, game, etc... are usually armed only with bows and arrows, and confine their outrages to stealing from the whites... though a few persons who have imprudently exposed themselves have been murdered. At this time, nearly all of them have been driven back some 20 or 30 miles into the mountains from which they occasionally [attack] the trains of pack mules, etc., transporting supplies for the miners in the interior.

The surgeon pointed out that so few Indians were captured, "that if we had no other way of becoming acquainted with the appearance, habits, manners, etc., of these aboriginal tribes, but very little would be known of them..."

Deyerle thought his physical surroundings were quite pleasant:

> Fort Humboldt... is located upon one of the most beautiful spots I have seen on the Pacific coast, having an unrivalled view of the bay and the broad waters of the Ocean in front stretching away to the westward — beautiful scenery on every hand — fine bodies of fertile land and elegant forests of the best lumber in the rear — surrounded with delicious flowering shrubs and plants — good water — agreeable climate — abundance of fish & game and indeed possesses all the elements necessary to make it in a time a delightful station, but notwithstanding all these things are very good in their way, I am not so well contented here as there is but little society and the country yet too much in its infancy to correspond with my tastes and inclinations.

By May, Dr. Deyerle was settling in but not satisfied with his predicament. He reported on his deep interest in plants and flowers and mentioned one of the important figures of California history:

I have been employing all the leisure time I can snatch from my practice — private and public — to the cultivation of a vegetable and flower garden. I have an excellent piece of ground, easily irrigated in summer, if it be required, and although the recent cool and wet weather retarded everything very much, yet within the last week, all my plants, etc., are beginning to look green and flourishing... I have planted 40 or 50 varieties of flower seeds, about a dozen of which were given me by a young lady friend in Benicia, and of familiar kinds, but the remainder came from the farm of old Capt. Sutter (whom you may recollect from the books was one of the original pioneers of California in 1840 — a Swiss by birth and once an officer in the French Army, in the time of Charles X) on Feather river, labeled in German names, and I cannot tell what they may turn out to be. Most of these latter seeds were brought from France, Germany and Switzerland some two years ago by Capt. St's family which came to join him after a separation of some 15 years.

By August 1853, some six months before Grant arrived, Deyerle was still living in a tent, tired of riding, fishing, and hunting and admitting that "no alternative is left me but to smoke my pipe and indulge in that indisputable prerogative of all soldiers — to grumble."

The young surgeon continued to express his boredom:

A very slight matter is sufficient to create interest, and like the time spent on a long sea-voyage when the appearance of a passing sail or even the flapping of a forlorn bird's wing, attracts universal attention, what would be deemed trifles in other places, here forms quite an event.

This understandable tendency to place great weight on small occurrences at a lonely outpost was the reason that U. S. Grant's tenure at Humboldt Bay was marked by innuendoes and rumors the remainder of his life.

Deyerle, in his early 30s, was a sensitive bachelor who did not take himself seriously and had a sense of humor and appreciated refinement and education. Like most Virginia gentlemen of his day, he enjoyed the company of ladies and was woefully disappointed in that respect with his new station:

> There is a little society on the Bay, but the life I expect to lead... will doubtless be rather a dull one...
> You must know, that everywhere in California, ladies are scarce, and especially so on Humboldt Bay, where among a population of nearly a thousand there are not more than 25 or 30 *women*, and not more than half a dozen *ladies* in that number.

Grant, six months later, wrote Julia that all the villages on the bay together had just about enough ladies "to get up a small sized Ball."[23]

The doctor reported more details on what it was like living on the bay during its earliest days.

> ...I wear (and have worn for several years) a moustache and beard because I choose to do it, because it is convenient, because it protects my mouth and face from the hot sun of summer, because it saves razors and because it is the general custom in California...

Although Grant had a beard for a short time in Mexico, it was on the Pacific Coast that he started the beard that was to stay with him through the Civil War. Grant grew his beard for the same reasons that Deyerle did his.

In a day of easy and rapid communication it is perhaps difficult for contemporary readers to understand the deep feelings of loneliness which the inhabitants of Fort Humboldt suffered through in the early 1850s. Months went by with no word from "the States."

Like Grant, almost a year later, the post surgeon, after living on beautiful, but lonely, Humboldt Bay for seven months, found no improvement in mail service.

---

[23]Grant, *Papers*, p. 317.

Dr. Deyerle became ill. His military service in Mexico and in interior California had made him susceptible to chills and fever. In his first Humboldt letters he wrote, "Today is rather cooler than usual, and writing in a tent without fire has benumbed my fingers, and the weather portending rain has exerted a saddening & stupifying influence upon me so that I cannot write." Three months later he complained about his health in a letter to his family in Virginia.

> The 'chills' is an old friend of mine; I had it several times in Mexico, and some half a dozen times since I have been in California, so that I have become about accustomed to its freaks. The period of actual suffering is short, but the most disagreeable feature about the disease is the feeling of languor, debility, low spirits and general 'malaise' which follow an attack, usually for several days.

These are the same feelings that Ulysses S. Grant had the next year at Fort Humboldt. Grant contracted the same ills in Mexico that Dr. Deyerle complained of and, like the post surgeon, had chills, low spirits and general feelings of depression following the attacks.

In the early morning of January 3, 1854, Captain Sam Grant boarded the *John S. McKim* in San Francisco harbor; sailing had been advertised for 10:00 a.m. The *McKim*, a small vessel, did not clear the harbor on schedule, but soon after was bucking and rolling in the rough January seas. After two stormy days the *McKim* delivered Grant to Humboldt Bay where he reported for duty.[24]

Grant's 250 mile trip from San Francisco seemed to him a long and tedious voyage.[25] It ended when he saw

[24]The author is indebted to John Haskell Kemble for identifying Grant's ship to Humboldt Bay. Dr. Kemble found the notations of harbor clearance and sailing in San Francisco papers of Jan. 3-4, 1854. [25]Grant, *Papers*, p. 315.

Fort Humboldt for the first time; "Grant reached this out-post of civilization where, with leaden skies overhead, mud and flood underfoot, the great bay on front and the dismal forest behind... he took up the petty duties and spirit-killing routine of garrison life."[26]

When Grant joined the 4th Infantry Detachment at Humboldt Bay, the rough, wooden Fort had been "finished" only a few months. Fourteen buildings had been constructed on the bluff on the bay's east side just outside Eureka. There were several small buildings for officers' quarters, an enlisted men's barracks, a commissary, hospital, powder house, laundry buildings, and a guard house. The buildings were grouped roughly around three sides of the 260-foot square parade ground which was open to the bay on the west side.

The buildings were all hand-hewed plank construction with most of them plastered inside. The officers' quarters were crude, with boards and barrels used for seats, some stuffed with moss and scraps of material. All was strictly frontier style. Rather an unimposing military post, it had no great fortifications, only some casually constructed earthwork. But progress had been made in a year.

Fort Humboldt was not unique among other forts in the frontier army. Few of them were stockaded or otherwise fortified; almost all were laid out with little thought of being a strong point to hold off an attack. There was usually no permanent, stone materials or skilled craftsmanship at these frontier installations, only hastily tossed-up patchworks of the local lumber.

One soldier wrote about such a post:

---

[26]Clara McGeorge Shields, "General Grant at Fort Humboldt in The Early Days," *Humboldt Times*, Eureka, Calif., Nov. 10, 1912 (cited hereafter as "Shields Article"). Almost all of this article is reprinted in *Ulysses S. Grant Assoc. Newsletter* of Apr., 1971.

Fort Humboldt, near Eureka, California.
Photograph taken by Vansant in the 1860s.

The buildings are built in a hollow square, leaving the center what is called a 'parade ground' where the military parades are held every morning. One side of the square is used as officers' quarters; the opposite side as a guard house, commisary department, offices, etc. The other two sides are soldiers' barracks. There is a flag staff in the center from which the stars and stripes flash and wave in the breeze. Out of this square are to be found a hospital, stable, yards, etc.[27]

At Humboldt Bay the Fort was largely a self-contained community with social life following a rather uninspired pattern.

It was not a particularly happy sight that awaited Grant when he arrived at Fort Humboldt. The log buildings looked as dreary as the small villages which were homes for the lumbermen and their sawmills. The entire scene was dominated by the dark, huge, dripping forest that came to the water's edge. Even worse was the fact that the commanding officer was the one Grant had had words with on at least two occasions ten years before in Jefferson Barracks.[28]

Life at this tiny frontier fort was boring and unbelievably dreary: bugle calls and drills, simple meals, drills, evening dress parade, drill, lowering of the flag and taps.

The only break in the routine was an occasional march to the mountains — trips that Grant anticipated eagerly. The military duties of the soldiers were to resolve such conflicts as they could, offer some measure of protection to the white families and hold prisoners from time to time.

[27]Robert M. Utley, *Frontiersman in Blue* (New York, 1967), p. 42.

[28]Buchanan and Grant had several run-ins which are documented. A lighter touch is captured by Shirley Seifert in her delightful novel, *Captain Grant,* which recounts (page 137) Captain Buchanan, president of the officers' mess at Jefferson Barracks, fining the young lieutenant on several occasions for being late to dinner. Grant had been visiting Miss Julia Dent at her home several miles away. Mrs. Seifert also creates words between the two on a parade ground during that same tour of duty and the indifferent greeting his new commanding officer gave him when Grant reported to Fort Humboldt.

The military life at Fort Humboldt was slow and monotonous: the Indians were not causing much trouble, and thus the mission of Company F lacked excitement. The lazy barracks life stifled the hopes of ambitious men. Some army officers could adjust to such a stupifying existence, but not Sam Grant. To the quiet and homesick soldier, Fort Humboldt was truly a hardship post. From the first day he began fighting a losing battle with boredom, he saw no escape from this unbearable condition — "he was flat on the ground."[29]

Homesick and increasingly discouraged with the army, his life became grayer and grayer. Grant was too down to break out of his lethargy. He was gloomy and could not motivate himself. Only when he re-read Julia's wrinkled letters received at Vancouver did his spirits lift and life seemed tolerable. As with most officers of the day, Grant's routine work was done by his subordinates so he had plenty of time to ride, gripe about the army, and lounge. He soon found his best lounging spots were Brett's Saloon and Ryan's Store. Only when he sipped whiskey there did he become lively and sociable, telling war stories of the Mexican conflict and then going outside to demonstrate his horsemanship to the settlers.[30]

Grant had an enviable characteristic even under the

[29]Colonel Nicholas Smith, *Grant, the Man of Mystery* (Milwaukee, 1909), p. 50.

[30]Several of Grant's biographers tell the story of his driving a strange rig — pell mell — through a village, presumable after having too much to drink. They report Capt. Sam driving three horses single file with a string of two or three buggies tied together and bumping along behind to the amazed delight of the villagers. W. E. Woodward, *Meet General Grant* (New York, 1928), p. 120, places this incident at Eureka; Lloyd Lewis, *op. cit.*, p. 326, and Richardson, *op. cit.*, p. 48 at Knight's Ferry. If this unlikely incident indeed did occur, I believe it was at Eureka. Knight's Ferry huddles on the side of a hill alongside the Stanislaus River and, of course, was the home of Grant's in-laws. The main street at Knight's Ferry does not lend itself to a straightaway run for such a colorful procession. Eureka's old main drag, however, meets the qualifications for such a parade and, of course, was the location of Ryan's Store.

duress of Fort Humboldt — he kept his temper under control. He seemed always to be frank, open and honest in his conduct toward others. Even while drinking he was a gentleman. Old-timers recalled Grant sitting on Ryan's wooden porch, staring at the dumpy, dripping little village and gazing at the dreariness all about him. Evenings were spent in card playing, reading or writing letters home and an occasional social gathering. Grant's four months at Fort Humboldt were dull and affected him deeply.

Grant had decided he did not like Fort Humboldt even before he saw it. In a letter to Julia from Fort Vancouver he called Humboldt, "a detestible place."[31] His ambitious friend, Lewis Hunt, had written to him at Fort Vancouver to say that he, Hunt, "was quite well but hartily tired of Humboldt Bay, or rather with the commanding officer there."[32] Even before he heard from Hunt, Grant indulged in some soldierly griping about Fort Humboldt's austerity in letters to his wife. Now, arriving at the bay, Grant thought it looked as bad as he feared and could not "say much in favor of the place." He was already beginning to feel boxed in. "Imagine a place closed in by the sea having thrown up two tongues of land, closed in a bay that can be entered only with certain winds," he wrote Julia.[33]

When Grant arrived there were only three other line officers present for duty; Buchanan, Hunt and the likable 1st Lt. Joseph Benson Collins.[34] Dr. Richard Potts had replaced Dr. Deyerle, and Brevet 2nd Lieutenant Alfred Eugene Latimer, out of West Point less than a year, had

---

[31]Grant, *Papers*, p. 306.
[32]*Ibid.*, p. 302.
[33]*Ibid.*, p. 315.
[34]*Ibid.*, p. 316.

not yet arrived. Except for Lt. Hunt, who could not escape, there had been a complete turnover of Fort Humboldt junior officers. Lt. Scott had resigned in May 1853, under the threat of court-martial, Lt. Underwood had been promoted and transferred to Fort Reading, and Lts. Bonnycastle and Crook had joined Captain Judah at Fort Jones in the mountains near Yreka, California. Grant, next to Lt. Col. Buchanan was the senior officer at the post.

Even though his new command was about one-third its authorized strength (there were less than 100 troops stationed at Fort Humboldt), Grant was pleased with Company "F," made up of old soldiers who knew how to keep themselves neat and out of trouble. He saw a familiar and friendly face, and chose A. P. Marple as his orderly. Private Marple had crossed the Isthmus and sailed in the *Golden Gate* with his Captain. Grant thought his company clearly a cut above "B" Company, whose ranks had been filled with recruits just as the 4th sailed for California.[35] Lt. Col. Buchanan was not quite as enthusiastic as Captain Grant about "F" Company. Prior to their new Captain's arrival, Buchanan reported their military appearance as only "fair," their discipline as "improving," and their instruction only "tolerable."[36]

After being at Fort Humboldt for less than a month, Grant was already sorely disturbed. He wrote his wife:

> You do not know how forsaken I feel here! The place is good enough but I . . . cannot help thinking about [my family] day and night . . . I [have] been separated from you. and Fred. long enough as to Ulys. I have never seen him . . . How very much I want to see all of you . . . I do nothing here but set in my room and read and occatsionally [sic] take a short ride . . .[37]

[35]*Ibid.*, p. 321.   [36]*Ibid.*, p. 322.   [37]*Ibid.*, p. 316.

Captain Grant was impressed, however, with the "dense forest of immense trees" and thought the view from the bluff, where his comfortable frame house sat, was outstanding. "We can look out of sea as far as the eye can extend."

Grant visited the four villages on the bay. Humboldt City and its 50 inhabitants did not impress him: "What they depend upon for support I do'nt know." He thought Bucksport "a flourishing little place of about 200," working hard at moving lumber to San Francisco. Eureka, he saw as just a bigger Bucksport with its 500 people. Those two towns loaded nineteen lumber vessels a month for San Francisco in early 1853, and several additional mills were being built that February.[38] By the next year, at least nine mills were operating on the bay, seven of them in Eureka.[39] Grant thought Union "the larges and best built town" and watched pack trains take provisions from there to the gold mines "and return with the dust."[40]

Social life at Humboldt Bay was not exactly spirited. The only officer's lady on the post was Mrs. Collins, but Dr. Pott's wife was expected shortly.

In 1904, one old settler who knew and admired the Captain at Humboldt, talked about Grant:

> I lived, at that time, [remembered Major Howard] on a ranch two miles from the fort and was acquainted with all the officers and they frequently visited my house. The first time I met Captain Grant was early one foggy morning soon after his arrival. Lieutenant Collins called at my home to borrow my gun to shoot ducks and he was accompanied by Captain Grant. Collins seemed to be showing the new comer around... I think [Grant] enjoyed the lively company of Collins, as he seemed to favor his society more than any of the other officers.

---

[38]*Ibid.*, p. 317.   [39]Coy, *op. cit.*, p. 118.   [40]Grant, *Papers*, p. 317.

F. S. Duff, who considered himself a close friend of Grant during Humboldt days, never heard Grant complain, "yet I could see that he was filled with an intense desire to be with his family... Many a stormy night when it was too dark to ride back to the Fort, did Captain Grant share my bed." Mr. Duff, who by 1854 owned a sawmill, lodging house, and a store, did quite a little business with the Fort and enjoyed many evenings with the officers there. In fact, he said, "It was my usual custom to drive down to the post Sundays and dine with them."

Duff noticed that Grant was not an enthusiastic sportsman and that even the officers who were became tired of hunting and fishing. He pointed out that at Humboldt Bay, in 1854, "there was no society in the ordinary sense of the word."

Another one of Grant's civilian friends was Dr. Jonathan Clark who temporarily assumed the medical duties at Fort Humboldt as the Army surgeons would come and go. It was Dr. Clark who attended Grant when he was ill in February and April of 1854. Years later Dr. Clark remembered and called those illnesses "severe attacks."[41]

Many of Grant's biographers exaggerated the length of time the young Captain spent at Fort Humboldt. In fact, he was there from January 5, to May 7, 1854, about four months. Several writers noted that during Grant's Humboldt tenure there was a great deal of rainy weather which made him despondent, but they have Grant arriving in October 1853 with most of the rainy season ahead.

During Grant's time at Humboldt Bay, not withstand-

---

[41] The recollections of Major Howard, F. S. Duff and Dr. Jonathan Clark quoted here are from the Shields' Article.

ing a general ill feeling between the Indians and the whites, there was no general Indian uprising. There was, however, some loss of life through attacks by the Indians, which usually were followed by retaliation from the other side.[42]

To those who remembered him at Fort Humboldt, Grant appeared to be an ordinary looking, rugged, but pleasant-faced young man. He was about five feet eight inches tall, with a large and straight nose, deep and steady eyes, firmly set mouth, and the short, rough, sandy beard he grew in Oregon. With his ruddy complexion and unsoldierly bearing he was not of the usual West Point mold. On his own time Grant usually wore canvas pants and coat topped with an old straw hat and a cigar or pipe in his mouth, entirely free from the stiff formalities of the service when off duty.[43] People who met him in those pioneer days thought him a quiet man, a better listener than a talker with reserved habits: not given to talking when there was no need.[44] Grant was recalled as an unassuming, shy, sober-minded and gentlemanly person, treating all with quiet courtesy.[45]

Lt. Col. Buchanan was remembered differently. Everyone agreed that Fort Humboldt's commanding officer was not universally popular. Private Marple thought that Buchanan was an efficient officer, strict in petty detail to the verge of absurdity. Clara McGeorge Shields talked with many early Humboldt Bay survivors in 1912, including Marple, Major Howard and F. S. Duff. She

---

[42]Coy, *op. cit.*, p. 143.

[43]N. S. Giberson, "Captain Grant's Old Post, Fort Humboldt," *The Overland Monthly*, Vol. VIII — Second Series, 1886, p. 136.

[44]D. L. Thornbury, *California's Redwood Wonderland*, (San Francisco, 1923), p. 70. The description of Grant at Humboldt Bay comes from Thornbury's excellent chapter, "Captain U. S. Grant."

[45]Shields' Article.

concluded that Buchanan was very punctilious and a
martinet. D. L. Thornbury wrote that Buchanan was too
strict in his discipline and too strong in his prejudices.[46]

One historian called Fort Humboldt the most dreary
and isolated billet, perhaps, in the United States.[47] To
relieve the situation Grant did enjoy the company of
several pioneer families and seemed especially fond of the
Duff, Heustis, Maloney, Dr. Jonathan Clark and James
T. Ryan families. It was Duff's big roan horse, Eclipse,
that he enjoyed riding most. On frequent occasions the
young captain would visit the Duff home in Eureka and
the Reverend Heustis' home in Bucksport. In 1922, the
Heustis' low, one-story house was still standing on a rise
in back of Bucksport where the south room was pointed
out to visitors as where the young captain had slept. It
was a cheery room, 12 x 10 feet, and 8 foot ceiling, one
little closet and two windows. One window overlooked
the bay and one faced south toward the Elk River Valley.

Grant's off-duty time at Fort Humboldt was spent
vainly trying to break the monotony of the life there. In
addition to visiting with civilian friends, he went into
Eureka to play pool or cards at the saloons, and wrote to
his family. When he could, the young captain would ride
in the countryside. There were practically no roads, but
he would ride Eclipse into the woods jumping over logs
for amusement. Years later, General Grant called him,
"the finest horse I ever saw west of the Rocky Mountains." His usual route was along a corduroy road which
went to a charcoal-making camp located at about Seventh
and G Streets in present-day Eureka.

---

[46]*Ibid.*, and Thornbury, *op. cit.*, p. 71.
[47]Leigh H. Iwine, *History of Humboldt County, California* (Los Angeles, 1915), p.
52.

Grant and other officers would stay overnight frequently at Duff's lodging house in Eureka. But there was
too little to do. Except for escort duty on the trails no
military expeditions were undertaken while Grant was at
Humboldt.

The road to Eureka from the Fort that Grant traveled
was a wide horse trail which passed close to the bluff on
one side and the mud flat, marshy edge of the bay on the
other. It roughly paralleled present-day Broadway. As it
got nearer the waterfront-downtown area, the roadway
became better as it eased into Front Street (First) and
Second Street, each but three or four blocks long. One
officer told of riding from Eureka to the Fort one night in
the mid-1850s;

> As he came near a small piece of woods his horse became
> suddenly restive and looking ahead he could see eye-balls
> glistening among the trees, and he realized that it was a pack of
> wolves. He spurred his horse, gave a loud yell and dashed
> through the wolves to safety of the open road.[48]

It was recorded that Grant enjoyed strolling out on
Buhne's point where Major Howard lived, just south of
the Fort, almost in line with the entrance to Humboldt
Bay. There he could see the breakers rolling in from two
directions, over the south shoals and from the northwest.
Spread out before him to the west and towards the north
lay the gray Pacific, reminding him of endless distances
and far away places. The specific location where Captain
Grant could view the ocean has disappeared and is not
now in existence.[49] Buhne's point has been eroded several

---

[48]Simpson Letters. This statement comes from Notes by Mary J. S. McCutchen,
daughter of surgeon Joseph Simpson and Mrs. Simpson, who was born at Fort
Humboldt in 1854.

[49]Irvine, *op. cit.*, p. 56.

hundred feet back, and the low sand dunes of the north peninsula have moved south to make the bay's entrance even more narrow. But the restless ebb and flow of the tide, and the vast expanse before him, can still send a chill of loneliness to the modern viewer. Grant began to brood about lack of news from his beloved wife. He was seriously disturbed about the poor mail service, and with each passing week it ate into him deeply:

> There is no regular mail between here and San Francisco so the only way we have of geting letters off is to give them to some Captain of a vessel to mail them after he gets down. In the same way mails are recieved. This makes it very uncertain...[50]

Mail service was always a problem. Several months after Grant had left Humboldt Bay, one army wife complained, "There is only one drawback to this post and that is the irregularity of the mails from San Francisco."[51]

Grant received only one letter from his wife during his entire stay at Fort Humboldt, and that letter was written in October 1853.

After only four weeks at his new post, Grant was physically sick and mentally at the end of his rope. He wrote Julia, "The state of suspense that I am in is scarsely bearable. I think I have been from my family quite long enough and sometimes I feel as through I could almost go home, with or without permission."

In early February he recorded, "I have been suffering for the last few days most terribly." He had a painful tooth extracted on February 5, leaving his face "swolen until it is as round as an apple and so tender that I do not feel as if I could shave... I could pass readily for a person

---

[50]Grant, *Papers*, p. 317.
[51]Simpson Letters.

of forty-five." Fort Humboldt Post Returns for February 1854, listed Grant as "sick."[52]

In early March he wrote his wife that he had not been a hundred yards from his door but once in the last two weeks. Grant recorded that he was tired and out of patience with Fort Humboldt.

> I have only had one letter from you in three months... [he wrote Julia] I sometimes get so anxious to see you, and our little boys, that I am almost tempted to resign (and obtain a position) where I can have you and them with me... Whenever I get to thinking upon the subject [of resigning without a job] however *poverty poverty* begin to stare me in the face....[53]

On March 25, 1854, Grant had about reached the end.

> I have had just one solitary letter from you since I arrived at this place and that was written about October of last year. I cannot believe that you have neglected to write all this time....
>
> The irregularity of mails is an annoyance which can only be appreciated by those who suffer from it....
>
> I do not feel as if it was possible to endure the separation much longer. But how do I know that you are thinking as much of me as I of you? I do not get letters to tell me so... Just think, by the time you recieve this Ulys. will be nearly two years old....[54]

Later, he was feeling better physically, but still he was despondent. "I have not been a quarter of a mile from my room for about a week." At the end of April, Fort Humboldt Post Returns list him as "sick" again.[55]

In northern California, as indeed elsewhere on the Pacific Coast, the high cost of living was very trouble-

[52]Grant, *Papers*, p. 321-22.

[53]*Ibid.*, p. 323.

[54]*Ibid.*, p. 326-27.

[55]*Ibid.*, p. 327-28.

some to the ordinary citizen. One budget-conscious Fort Humboldt wife recorded that in June 1854, eggs were $1.25 a dozen, butter .75-$1.00 a pound, chicken $3.00 a piece and a good cow cost $150.00.[56] Grant wrote, "Living here is extravigantly high besides being very poor." When Potts arrived, Grant, Dr. Potts, and Lt. Col. Buchanan tried messing together. That arrangement cost Grant "about $50 per month... including servant hire and washing." Later, Grant moved over to be with Lewis Hunt who could stand no arrangement that included his commanding officer.

Grant's tenuous financial condition can be imagined from the following presentation. From June 1853, his pay and total cash available was going down, but his Humboldt expenses were up. And at Humboldt Bay he had less opportunity for business ventures than he did at his previous West Coast duty station.

U. S. Grant's Pay Record

	Fiscal Year Ending June 1852	Fiscal Year Ending June 1853	Fiscal Year Ending June 1854
Pay	$ 480	$ 677	$ 536
Rations	366	365	438
Allowances for Servants	193	171	187
Forage	288	328	140
Fuel	58	74	7
Quarters	16		
Baggage Transportation	60	13	262
Per Diem (Courts Martial)	9		16
	$1,470	$1,628	$1,586

In August 1853, Grant was promoted to Captain, yet his pay for the fiscal year dropped. Likewise, two of his

---

[56]Simpson Letters.

brother officers also stationed on the West Coast suffered pay cuts in that same period: Captain Wallen's pay decreased from $795 for fiscal year 1853 to $510 in fiscal year 1854 and Captain Alvord's from $811 to $582. Lloyd Lewis speculated that the extra pay given for Pacific service was withdrawn by the War Department in 1853 and not paid in 1854:

> All of which makes me wonder if, in addition to the high cost of living on the Coast, this actual shrinkage of income, even though he was promoted, did not hasten his decision to resign. If so, this is a fact that no previous published biography has brought out, and seems important to me.[57]

U. S. Grant 3rd recorded that his grandfather's low army pay prevented him from bringing his wife and children to the Pacific Coast. Grant 3rd believed that the "resignation was a natural decision arrived at after considerable consideration... His father-in-law, with whom his wife and children were forced to live, had always wanted him to resign and was probably constantly needling [Julia] to get him to resign and come home."[58]

Grant was always taciturn, quiet, not prone to speak out on trivial matters. In such an unhappy environment, he turned more inward to search for resources which he did not have. He needed someone to share his hopes and the burden of his anxieties. He found no one at Fort Humboldt, no solace from the grim surroundings and the frigid relationship he had with his commanding officer.

[57] Information on Grant's pay comes from an exchange of letters between Lloyd Lewis and U. S. Grant 3rd; copies in the Lloyd Lewis Papers, U. S. Grant Assoc., Carbondale, Ill. Lewis to Grant 3rd, Dec. 28, 1948. Grant 3rd to Lewis, Feb. 11, 1949. Lewis notes that U. S. Grant's pay record comes "from the House Documents' publication of army registers and each officers' pay."

[58] Ulysses S. Grant 3rd letter to Lloyd Lewis, Feb. 11, 1949.

Grant learned a great deal about himself at Fort Humboldt. He determined, finally, that a routinized, humdrum existence which did nothing to quicken his blood or stir his senses was not for him. The indomitable general of later years came to the conclusion in the redwood forests of California, somewhat reluctantly, that army life was unacceptable. There was no spirit of patriotic duty, no compulsion to repay the education his country had given him, and no other compelling reason for him to stay. The army seemed to offer only security and genteel poverty. Although he appreciated that security, and he worried terribly about what the future held, the cost was too great. He knew not how he would make his way in the world with his wife, not known for her thrift, and two little boys, but he had to break out of the morosity plaguing him.

Grant learned something else on Humboldt Bay. He found out where he did *not* fit; and, that was a gain. It is possible that his understanding of himself and the realization that he could not be a whole man without the comfort and closeness of his family stirred the process of making him a great man.

Grant discovered that unless he was busy and fully-occupied, he needed his family close about him. Also, and most importantly for his future, he realized that he could organize, give orders, manage organizations, and projects better than he could take orders so detailed and insipid that they stultified his creative leadership.

If Grant had been the commanding officer at Fort Humboldt, which he thought would be the case, would the story have been different? Undoubtedly yes. One cannot help but imagine the energy and effort that commanding officer Grant would have put into establishing a mail service from San Francisco to Humboldt Bay, compared to Buchanan's feeble effort.

Humboldt Bay may have been the most disappointing time of Grant's life: worse than his time as a farmer; worse than his months as an agent; even worse than dull days as a leather clerk in Galena.

Maybe Humboldt Bay forced him into a radical change of lifestyle, those changes of building his Hardscrabble cabin, physical outdoor work, open air, family voices almost always within earshot, and quiet comforting evenings with Julia. Perhaps these things, forced by life at Humboldt Bay, pushed Grant into finding himself and prepared him for his trial by fire and steel.

Grant summed up that Fort Humboldt "would be a good enough place but the suspense I am in would make paradice form a bad picture."[59] In his *Memoirs*, written during the last days of his life, he would not find it possible to mention his northern California days.

---

[59]Grant, *Papers*, p. 320.

Chapter VI

Resignation:
"Accepted as Tendered," Jefferson Davis

On April 11, 1854, Grant's formal commission as Captain arrived. After ten years as a First Lieutenant and five years as a Brevet Captain, this event was enough to push Grant to final action. He resigned from the United States Army.[1] No spur of the moment impulse nor embarrassing incident provoked the decision. He had written his wife that he was considering resigning at least four times since arriving at Fort Vancouver.[2] After much thought Grant made his move.

On the day that the commission arrived, Grant wrote two letters: the first he sent to the War Department acknowledging his commission, the second went to Lt. Col. Buchanan, tendering his resignation effective July 31, 1854. Buchanan endorsed a speedy recommendation that same day. Major General John E. Wool, Commander

[1] Grant was actually promoted to Captain by Secretary Davis on Aug. 9, 1853. President Franklin Pierce did not sign the formal commission paper, however, until Feb. 9, 1854. Grant, *Papers*, p. 312.

[2] Grant, *Papers*, pp. 278, 300, 320 and 323. The dates of these letters were Dec. 19, 1852, June 15, 1853, Feb. 6, 1854, and Mar. 6, 1854.

of the Department of the Pacific, approved and forwarded the resignation to the War Department eleven
days later; Major General Winfield Scott's headquarters
in Washington noted its acceptance on May 26. And on
the 2nd of June, 1854, Jefferson Davis, Secretary of War,
endorsed Grant's resignation "Accepted as tendered."[3]

The official notes added to Grant's letter indicated that
Grant had his accounts and records in good order, that he
owed nothing to the government, and that no fault could
be assigned to his performance of duty. The original
Grant resignation file is now in the National Archives
and shows nothing but army routine notations. Hamlin
Garland studied the file in the Adjutant-General's office
in Washington D.C. in early 1897. He summarized:

> It will thus be seen that Capt. Grant not only went out of the
> service with his accounts in order but that no hint of his reasons
> for leaving the service appears in the Adjutant-General's office.
> His motives are stated to be unknown to the office. This settles
> two or three of the stories which have gone the rounds as
> gossip. Whatever may have induced him to send in his
> resignation nothing against his good name ever appeared in the
> office of the Adjutant-General.[4]

Grant was neither happy nor healthy at Fort Humboldt, and he resigned for several reasons.

The formal notification of his promotion reminded
him vividly that advancement in the peacetime army was
excruciatingly slow. He now knew it would be years, if
ever, before he could provide a lifestyle that his wife Julia
was accustomed to and desired, and that he wanted to

---

[3]*Ibid.*, pp. 328-30, Jefferson Davis wrote these words as an endorsement to Grant's
Apr. 11, 1854, resignation letter.

[4]"Grant's Resignation," Feb. 10, 1897. Garland Papers. The author also studied
the Grant resignation file in the Nat. Arch.

give her. He was desperately lonely on the West Coast. One Fort Humboldt wife hit the mark when she observed, "Many officers in these out of way posts seem to find time hangs so heavy on their hands."[5] Even at Fort Vancouver, when he had congenial companions and more comfortable circumstances, Grant thought of resigning and going back to Missouri or Ohio to farm, or going into business on the Pacific Coast. The days at Fort Humboldt were worse. With a nagging commanding officer, more time on his hands, and slower mails to contend with, Grant's loneliness and desperation increased.

The cost of living was so terribly high that bringing his family to the Pacific did not seem practical. His salary was inadequate, it would take too much time for him to establish profitable sideline ventures, and he wanted to be with his family. And Grant was not well. He suffered from migraine headaches; chills and fever eroded his resolve and left him weak and dispirited.

Grant's morale was low when the promotion letter arrived, and he decided the time had come. Even after making that decision, he remained ill. It was not until May 7, 1854, that Capt. Grant could finish his routine reports, pull himself together, and abandon Fort Humboldt. Grant was so anxious to be on his way that he left before he was notified officially that his resignation had been accepted.

The last time I saw Grant [said Major Howard] was just before his departure. One morning I was going to Eureka and at the foot of the hill where the road turns toward the post, I met Captain Grant and Lieutenant Collins. They were in a buggy

---

[5]Simpson Letters.

and Grant's face was partially hidden by a high coat-collar. He did not notice my salutation which was returned by Collins. [It will be recalled Grant was ill at that time.][6]

Grant requested, and was granted, sixty days leave with permission for an extension to take him to July 31 so that he could finish his paperwork. Lt. Col. Buchanan recommended that the leave be granted: "Capt. Grant has important papers and vouchers necessary to the settlement of his accounts, at Fort Vancouver, and wishes time to collect and arrange them."[7] Grant was relieved from the "F" Company duties and replaced by Lewis Hunt, but on May 1, Buchanan wrote to the Pacific Department headquarters, "Captain Grant is too unwell to travel just yet,... but will proceed to San Francisco by the first steamer."[8]

Grant wrote to Julia that it would probably take between May 31 to June 15 to complete his public business and wind up the private investments he had underway. Although Grant thought he should go to Fort Vancouver to close out his accounts properly, he told Julia he would not go unless the government paid his way.[9] There is no record that he went back to Washington Territory at that time.

That Grant may have erred in not doing so is indicated by the persistence of the military bureaucracy. Auditors in Washington, D.C. pestered Grant in Missouri during 1855, 1856, and 1857 about vouchers, receipts, corrections, and bookkeeping entries which were needed to square Fort Vancouver records. On May 25, 1857, three

[6]Shields' Article.
[7]Lt. Col. Buchanan to Maj. E. D. Townsend, Apr. 11, 1854. Grant, *Papers*, p. 331.
[8]*Ibid.*, May 1, 1854. Grant, *Papers*, p. 332.
[9]Grant, *Papers*, pp. 331-33.

years after he left Fort Humboldt, War Department officials wrote that he must secure his commanding officer's signature before final settlement could be made. They pointed out helpfully that "Col. Bonneville is now stationed at Santa Fe, New Mexico."[10]

For years the accepted story of Grant's time at Fort Humboldt concluded with his resignation from the army in disgrace. That story, with minor variations, went along the following lines.

The young captain was quiet and withdrawn, much preoccupied with a melancholy longing to be with his children and his lively wife of five years. With little to do, he became even more withdrawn, aching for his family, brooding always about how to support them on less than $100 a month.

As was the case with most soldiers of his day, Grant drank too much, spending much of his time in James Ryan's establishment in Eureka. That behavior was not long in coming to the attention of Colonel Buchanan.

Buchanan did not like Grant. He did not like him at Jefferson Barracks and he did not like him at Fort Humboldt. The colonel began to think that Grant was ill-fitted for a military career. Buchanan did not want inefficient, slovenly, and drunken officers in his regiment. He spoke to Grant about his habits, telling him in effect, to "shape up or ship out." Grant agreed to try to improve and, for a time, did so. But eventually Grant "fell off the wagon" and one day, while paying off his company, fell out of Buchanan's limited good graces. He appeared to be intoxicated and the whole regiment saw the incident.

[10]Captain Marcus De Lafayette Simpson to Ulysses S. Grant, May 25, 1857. Nat. Arch. Wash., D.C. Record Group 192, Letters Sent.

This was enough for straight-laced Robert Buchanan. A resignation was called for and delivered.[11]

There is much truth in this tale about Grant's loneliness, his dislike of the commanding officer, and time spent in Eureka saloons. It is also true that Captain Grant could not hold his liquor well, and a little whiskey went a long way with him. The implications that he was a drunkard and resigned from the army at Buchanan's insistence must be carefully examined. Some allege that Buchanan held an undated, but signed resignation from Grant to keep him in line. A review of Grant's correspondence from the West Coast, particularly his official letter of resignation and requests for leave, is inconsistent with such a theory.[12] He had been thinking about resigning for a long time and had corresponded with Julia about that decision beginning in December 1852.

The most enduring tale about the reputation and character of Ulysses Grant concerned his drinking habits. Many of his biographers, political enemies, and friends, traced his alleged weakness for liquor back to pre-Civil War days on the West Coast.

What follows is an attempt to put Grant's drinking into a perspective: an effort to capture various shadings of opinion which represent, in the main, the large body of "evidence" that has been collected, both pro and con, over many years.

In preparation for his respected articles and biography

---

[11] This general tone and description of Grant at Humboldt Bay comes from several of his biographers; for example, Woodward, *op. cit.*, his chapter nine; Bruce Catton, *U. S. Grant and the American Military Tradition* (New York, 1954), pp. 49-51; Lewis, *op. cit.*, pp. 324-31; King, *op. cit.*

[12] Grant, *Papers*, p. 329. Dr. Simon footnotes: "The document [Grant's Apr. 11, 1854 resignation] is inconsistent with accounts that . . . Buchanan had previously held an undated resignation."

of Grant, Hamlin Garland interviewed former Commissary-General Robert McFeely:

> I was in the 4th Regiment with Grant. I was at Fort Vancouver... Grant drank very little on the Coast... One-twentieth part of what the other officers consumed showed on him... Grant was not a drunkard. Liquor seemed a virulent poison to him, and yet he had a fierce desire for it. One glass would show on him, and two or three would make him stupid.[13]

Drum Major James Elderkin gave Garland colorful and contradictory information:

> His habits at Fort Vancouver were very regular. He drank considerably there. He had to leave the army there at Humboldt Bay... His wife was always in the eastern states and I think that had a great deal to do with his drinking... I never saw him under the influence of liquor in my life. All I know about that is what I heard people say. I heard them say that he drank at Fort Vancouver, but not to excess.[14]

Henry C. Hodges, who joined the 4th Infantry in 1851 after graduating from West Point, met Grant in May 1852. Hodges was posted to Fort Vancouver but not Fort Humboldt. He did not see Grant from the spring of 1853 until the fall of 1863, but he always considered himself an admirer and a friend of Grant's. Hodges responded to William C. Church's request for information before Church wrote his biography of Grant.

> Of course it is well known that General Grant drank now and then, but he was not, as has been often charged, by any means a drunkard. He would perhaps go on two or three sprees a year, but was always open to reason, and when spoken to on

---

[13] Garland Papers.

[14] *Op. cit.* McFeely and Elderkin were both at Fort Vancouver not Fort Humboldt. These quotations are from Garland's notes; he did not use them in his book.

the subject would own up and promise to stop drinking which he did...

[When McClellan's expedition was being outfitted at Fort Vancouver] Grant got on one of his little sprees, which annoyed and offended McClellan exceedingly, and in my opinion he never quite forgave Grant for it...

The resignation was brought about in this way; his commanding officer [was] a very good officer, but a martinet and 'sot in his ways.' It seems that one day while his company was being paid off, Captain Grant was at the pay table slightly under the influence of liquor. This coming to the knowledge of Colonel Buchanan he gave Grant the option of resigning or having charges against him; Grant resigned at once...[15]

Colonel Church wrote to Hodges on January 5, 1897: "Do you think Grant drank much when he was in civil life or after he [entered] the Army again?" Hodges answered two days later:

Grant in civil life undoubtedly drank, but not to any great extent I imagine, as he went into the war with unimpaired faculties. He also drank some in the second period of his Army life, but not enough to do any harm — and for years before his death he did not drink at all. He was a grand man and if he did drink a trifle it hurt nobody...[16]

As an old man in 1915, Hodges, writing from Pasadena, California congratulated Charles King for his recent book on U. S. Grant and reminisced:

The General was not a drinking man, as that term is understood but now and then, before he left the Regiment, he would get on a 'spree.' When some one of his friends would tell him he was drinking & that he ought to knock off, he would own up & say he would stop, and would stop right off.[17]

[15]Hodges (Church Papers), undated but just prior to Jan. 5, 1897.

[16]Ibid., Jan 7, 1897.

[17]Henry C. Hodges to Charles King, Mar. 21, 1915. The Charles King Papers of the State Hist. Soc. of Wisc., Madison, Wisc.

Granville O. Haller of Pennsylvania was a Brevet Major in the 4th Infantry. He did not accompany Bonneville across the Isthmus, but was in charge of moving two companies around Cape Horn. Although not stationed at Fort Humboldt, Haller was with Grant at other posts. He wrote to Church in 1897 that Grant not only drank frequently but "had the habit of drinking in a peculiar way." Haller described Grant as a four-fingered drinker of straight whiskey, gulping large tumblers of liquor, "more or less frequently each day, according to his mingling more or less with boon companions. The habit had become confirmed with him."[18]

In 1928 U. S. Grant, Jr., writing to his nephew, U. S. Grant 3rd, struck a provocative note:

> For your own information I will tell you that during the Wilderness Campaign your grandfather was a teetotaler and that his staff never drank about Hdqts. Robert Lincoln affirmed this of his own knowledge stating that he was on Genl Grant's staff as a volunteer aid during that campaign... Your grandfather abstained from alcoholic drinks for exactly the same reason your father did and you know your father was a total abstainer...[19]

Grant's old butler and valet Harrison Terrell, who

---

[18]Granville O. Haller to William C. Church, Mar. 17, 1897. Church Papers. In 1863 Haller was dismissed from the army on the charge of disloyal sentiments. The allegation was unsupported and unfounded but it took Major Haller until 1878 for the House of Representatives to give him an opportunity to vindicate his loyalty. Grant as Secretary of War and later as President did not go out of his way to help Haller. Considering what Grant did for some of his old army friends, there is something unusual about the Haller affair. Major Haller's damaging letter of 1897 may have been affected by Grant's apparent indifference to his plight. (House of Representatives Report No. 375, 45th Congress, 2nd Session, Mar. 11, 1878.)

[19]U. S. Grant, Jr., to U. S. Grant 3rd, Nov. 17, 1928. U. S. Grant Papers, Special Collections/Morris Library, Southern Illinois Univ., Carbondale, Illinois. The reader can supply his own interpretation, but the author believes that both Grant and his son Fred could not hold their liquor well, were aware of it, and conducted themselves accordingly.

served him during the last years of his life, knew why Grant did not drink much. Terrell explained that Grant drank very little alcohol because of a weak stomach. "Two drinks of a couple of small swallows each was as much as he ever ventured upon a sitting, and even this small quantity would" slur his speech. Knowing this, Grant very seldom drank more than one or two drinks in an evening. Terrell also recorded that Grant never drank wine or liquor of any kind "in moments of excitement or in any crisis."

> It is not true that Gen. Grant was a whiskey guzzler. Like many another man, he liked an occasional nip very well, but, after all, he was no more than a moderate drinker... [From] personal observation of Gen. Grant's habits... I am confident that he was not drinking to excess, or to hurt his judgment...[20]

Captain Schenck, some twenty-eight years after the incident, related an anecdote about Grant's drinking on board the *Ohio* during the passage to Panama.

> I always recollect in connection with this acquaintance with Lieutenant Grant that he had an excellent taste for good liquors. I had given him the liberty of the sideboards in my cabin, and urged him frequently never to be backward in using it as though it were his own, and he never was. Every night after I turned in, I would hear him once or twice, sometimes more, open the door quietly and walk softly over the floor so as not to disturb me; then I would hear the clink of the glass, and a gurgle, and he would walk softly back.[21]

Col. Isaac Stewart who served under Grant for several years, gave an interview to *The New York World* at the Hotel Astor on August 6, 1885:

---

[20] *The New York Sun*, May 3, 1903. Special Collections/Morris Library, Southern Illinois Univ., Carbondale, Ill.

[21] *Dayton Ohio Daily Journal*, Jan. 27, 1880. Is it possible that others among the ship's company knew where the Captain kept his whiskey?

There has been no little amount of talk attmepting to prove that
Gen. Grant was a drinking man. I know he wasn't. Of course,
he might take a glass, just as you and I would, but he was not by
any means addicted to drink. I only saw him take one glass of
whiskey during the [Civil] war . . . It was a whopping big drink
and the only one I ever saw the General take during the years I
was with him. If Gen. Grant did drink, certainly no one ever
knew it. He was always calm, quiet and self-possessed, whether
in the peak of conflict or after the battle . . . [22]

Thomas Anderson, who followed Lewis Cass Hunt as
commander of Fort Vancouver after the Civil War, was a
regimental commander in Buchanan's brigade in the
Army of the Potomac during the campaign of 1862.
(Anderson was not at Fort Humboldt nor in the army
before the Civil War. He became a general officer during
the Philippine Insurrection.) Anderson wrote that he was
"very intimate with Col. Buchanan & had my first
information as to the Humboldt episode and also of his
retirement from him."

From Fort Vancouver, where he had taken an interest
in Grant's West Coast sojourn, Anderson answered
Hamlin Garland:

[Buchanan] gave Genl then Captain Grant the option of
resigning or standing trial under the charge of drinking on
duty . . . [In] a conversation I had with him [Hunt] in 1880 he
confirmed in the main Buchanan's statement to me about the
arrest & resignation of Grant.

The particulars I gave about his Grants being put in arrest at
a Sunday morning Inspection, I received from some officers of
this Post who messed with Col. Hunt here & had the statement
from him before his death. One of these officers . . . told me last
night, that his remembrance is that Hunt told him that the last
occasion on which he put Grant in arrest by Buchanan order
was when Grant attended the payment of his company in full
uniform . . .

[22]*The New York World*, Aug. 7, 1885.

I remember absolutely, that Col. Buchanan told me distinctly that he had condoned a similar offense in Grant before he forced, or as he said, *permitted* his resignation as a favor... Grants most intimate & life long friend was Genl Rufus Ingalls. They lived together in the same house here... I have had many talks with Ingalls about Grants service & life in this part of the country. He was not at Humboldt where Grant got into his trouble, but he had heard the same account of the matter that I had & never disputed the facts, but claimed that Grant was not so intoxicated but what he could have done duty & would have been acquitted if tried but would not stand trial to save his wife's feelings. His version was that Buchanan, then the senior Captain of the Regiment was prejudiced against Grant & was an infernal old martinette & a d--a old S. of a B. & other explitives of the same elegant characters.

There is a gentleman in the adjoining town of Vancouver, named Lewis Sohns, a man now of wealth & fine character who was here as a Band Musician when Grant was Post Quartermaster. He says while here, that Grant was a hard drinker, but not a drunkard... That he was always dignified and self contained. Maj. Theodore Eckerson yet living in Portland gives the same account of him & from general report tradition I knew it is true...[23]

Outspoken Eunice Tripler wrote her impressions of army drinking habits and commented on a few officers who reached high rank.

In the old army, after the business of each day, many of the older officers were accustomed to give themselves to drink — it was a dreadful example to those younger, who didn't like to be called 'milk-sops.' It would be said of a man, 'He is not a drinking man. He is never drunk before dinner.' It seemed that all that could be expected of a man was that he should keep sober in the morning. Common descriptive terms were 'a one-bottle man,' 'a two-bottle man.'

In California Dr. Tripler was associated with U. S. Grant, W. T. Sherman, Joseph Hooker, E. D. Townsend. Hooker, at

---

[23]Thomas Anderson to Hamlin Garland, Aug. 15, 1896. Garland Papers.

this time, was a gambler and drunkard. Grant was in my husband's care and Dr. Tripler was entirely frank and open in dealing with his case. He, at last, resigned from the Army and came East. From the difference in rank, first in Dr. Tripler's favour and later in Grant's there was hardly intimacy between the two.[24]

In the early 1900's local historians talked with old residents and their descendants, and reported on Grant's career in Humboldt County.

...it has been discovered in almost every instance that some of the traditions affecting Grant's private life lack evidential corroboration, being based on ancient and shadowy rumor.[25]

Clara McGeorge Shields wrote in 1912 that "this theory [Grant resigning under pressure] is erroneous, as the most careful investigation among those associated with him at Fort Humboldt [proves]." She talked with Grant's old and trusted orderly A. P. Marple who denied that there was any special cause for Grant's resignation, other than that he was not satisfied with existing conditions. Grant felt his life was being wasted, according to Marple, and that Grant's circumstances were decidedly unpleasant.[26]

Before the turn of the century Marple became the Keeper of the Cape Mendocino lighthouse and lived to be one of the oldest settlers in Humboldt County. Marple passed along some of his experiences of early Fort Humboldt to a local reporter, to Major E. G. Underwood's widow, and talked with Mrs. Shields before he died in 1912. Marple's reminiscences are singular, and they do not record Grant as a drunk. Prejudiced in favor

[24]Eunice Tripler, *Some Notes of Her Personal Recollections.* (New York, 1910), pp. 82, 109, 111-12.
[25]Irvine, *op. cit.*, p. 52.
[26]Shields' Article.

of his commander he may have been, but Marple made no move to sensationalize Grant's character or his habits.[27]

D. L. Thornbury wrote in 1923 that there were many false stories concerning Grant's drinking habits. "In order to have actually committed all the breaches of sobriety credited to him by the stories I have personally heard, he would have had to live in Humboldt four years and to do nothing else."

> A great deal of tradition has naturally grown up concerning his stay in Humboldt... Most of the local stories are absolute fiction, as no man could possibly have done all attributed to him in the short space of seven months. [Not to mention four months!]

Thornbury reported, "It is hard to get at the facts when giving a history of those [Fort Humboldt] months." He records Grant as unassuming, shy and sober-minded, attracting little attention, giving all indications that he would soon be forgotten.[28]

In 1931, Will N. Speegle, Eureka newspaper editor and writer, wrote that it was Grant's practice to visit Eureka frequently and that he spent time at "Billy Brett's saloon on Front Street near F ... But it is not unlikely that the stories of his participation in the early day drinking are greatly exaggerated."[29] Later, Mr. Speegle wrote that at "the famous R. W. Brett saloon on First Street [Grant] sat and listened to local gossip but did little talking himself."[30]

Martha B. Roscoe, charter member and past president

---

[27]Fountain Papers, *op. cit.*, pp. 211-213 and p. 246; A. P. Marple letters to *West Coast Signal*, Sept. 7, 1876 and June 5, 1878. Also, letter written to Marple by Mary B. Underwood, July 22, 1881, Fountain Papers, p. 233. Clara McGeorge Shields talked with the old settler just before he died in 1912: Shields' Article.

[28]Thornbury, *op. cit.*, pp. 69-70 and 73.

[29]*Humboldt Times*, Dec. 17, 1931.

[30]Fountain Papers, p. 257.

of the Humbolt County Historical Society was named "Historian of the Year" in 1977, her 82nd year. She was chosen on the basis of her unflagging interest in historical events of Humboldt County and her painstaking recording of those events.

Mrs. Roscoe pointed out that Brett's establishment was even called "Brett's Court" in those early days since all the political leaders, and the people who ran Humboldt County, got together there to meet informally and to settle issues. She concluded from her research that "U. S. Grant was not a sot. He associated, in his off-hours with well-respected Dr. Jonathan Clark, J. T. Ryan, Reverend A. J. Huestis, and others who were recognized as the leading citizens in the area. They were not boozers and they were his friends." Mrs. Roscoe continued, "I have talked personally with old timers who know the facts... I knew two of Ryan's nephews, one was 18 when the elder Ryan died... and they all discounted stories of U. S. Grant the drunk."[31]

In 1951, Andrew Genzoli, one of Humboldt County's respected newspapermen and historians, wrote that some of the stories about Fort Humboldt's early days were "enjoyable if you aren't acquainted with the historical scene." Mr. Genzoli complained of old worn out myths about Captain Grant and one unproved incident. "Someday," he wrote, "someone will write our stories as they should be written."[32]

In the *History of Humboldt County*, published in 1915, Leigh H. Irvine concludes:

> That he was not an abstainer seems clear beyond dispute. There is grave doubt, however, whether he ever drank to the

[31]Interview with Martha Roscoe, Oct. 11, 1979, Eureka, Calif.
[32]*Humboldt Times*, Nov. 25, 1951.

extent ascribed by some of the rumors that have been exaggerated during the last half century. A vast amount of cloudy tradition has grown up regarding his stay at Humboldt.[33]

During the 1930s the citizens of Eureka and Humboldt County joined each year during the Fourth of July season to celebrate "The Days of General Grant." A 1937 Humboldt Times article stated that there was no other locality which could claim the early day residency of a man who not only saved his nation but who afterwards became its president.

The article, "When Captain in U. S. Army, Great Man Was at Fort Humboldt," reported that Captain Grant's stay in the county was filled with experiences which were set down in local history, but because Grant spent most of his time brooding over the fate that deposited him on Humboldt Bay, he did not refer to those days in his *Memoirs*. Bad winter weather (the article, incorrectly, had him arriving in October 1853), coupled "with his lonesomeness and his inability to fraternize with the commandant of the post, made things unpleasant and so in 1854 he resigned from the army and returned east to his family."

This article confirms that Grant found consolation in the friendship of Dr. Jonathan Clark and visited the Clark home frequently. Clark family history recorded frequent visits by Captain Grant and credited him with being a fine young man with characteristics that gave promise of a great career.

Grant and his friends would meet "at the William Brett saloon on First street, and this gave rise to the stories that one hears of his carousing while here. Those who know the inside of the story, however, brand such stories as

[33] Irvine, *op. cit.*, p. 53.

without foundation." The *Humboldt Times* article pointed out that "His visitations at the Brett saloon were much
after the manner of men's associations with pals at their
club. At that time the Brett Saloon was about the only
congregating place in what was then an embryo lumber
camp."

> Dreary as Grant's life in Fort Humboldt must have been, he
> retained a friendly spirit toward those who were his friends
> here and in later years greeted [them] with warmth and
> affection.[34]

It is appropriate at this time to weigh some of this
contradictory testimony.

Grant drank, sometimes to excess, but he was not a
problem drinker. His physical build made it impossible
for him to drink much, yet he had sometimes desired
alcohol to relieve his loneliness. Grant did spend time in
Eureka saloons, but that is not evidence of heavy
drinking. Here is where community leaders met, talked
about a wide variety of subjects, and expressed the
civilized conviviality of that isolated place.

Did Buchanan insist upon his resignation following an
incident at the pay table? Probably not. The reports are
conflicting, and we cannot be sure how much of that
account belongs to the category of California myths
about Grant, and how much Buchanan reported later
when Grant achieved fame. Buchanan made Grant
uncomfortable, but the Captain made his own decision at
a time of his own choice.

At this date, so far removed from the time in question,
it is impossible to know whether the payroll episode did
indeed take place. Some say it did, and others say it did

---

[34]"When Captain in U. S. Army, Great Man Was at Fort Humboldt," *Humboldt Times*, Mar. 21, 1937.

not. That Grant and his fellow officers drank off-duty seems to be undisputed. That Grant was drunk on duty has not been proven. Regarding Grant's health, and especially his migraine headaches, John Y. Simon observed, "doctors nowdays are paying more attention to the psychological cause of such an ailment and the type of person who has it. And the headaches and the malaria together or singly could mislead observers into thinking that a man was suffering the ravages of excessive drinking."[35]

The only valid conclusion that can be drawn about Grant's drinking is that he drank — like most soldiers of his time. But he was not a drunkard. Grant did not consume large quantities of liquor because his body did not require much to achieve the inevitable results. Some of Grant's contemporaries recorded that he went on "sprees," but none accused him of failing in his duty because he was under the influence.

It was ironic that hard-drinking Henry M. Judah, a classmate at West Point, took Grant's place at Fort Humboldt. Judah and Grant had agreed to exchange posts. Grant was to escape Buchanan by moving to Fort Jones on the Scott River, near Yreka in the mountains of northern California, while Judah would accept a transfer to Fort Humboldt. Grant received orders to go to Fort Jones on June 10, 1854 — a month after he resigned. The order was later canceled. Judah's reputation with the bottle was legendary. George Crook recalled a short skirmish with Indians above Fort Jones in early 1854 in which Judah was so drunk he had to be lifted from his horse.[36] Buchanan undoubtedly got the worst of the deal when Judah later joined his command.

---

[35]John Y. Simon to the author, July 8, 1977.
[36]Crook, *Autobiography*, p. 7, and pp. 19-20.

Just after Grant departed in the summer of 1854, the army's Inspector General Colonel Joseph K. F. Mansfield came to look at Fort Humboldt for the War Department. He found four officers present for duty: Lt. Col. Buchanan, Captain Henry M. Judah, now Grant's replacement as Company "F" commander, 1st Lt. Hunt, and Dr. Simpson. Other assigned officers, 1st Lt. Collins and 2nd Lt. Latimer, were not there. The total force at Fort Humboldt had shrunk to 66.

Colonel Mansfield was quite complimentary of Lt. Col. Buchanan and his command. He thought Buchanan's siting of the post excellent: "well selected in rear of the town, and on high ground, and commands a good view of the harbor and its entrance." He was especially impressed with the size of the 640-acre reservation, "thus securing wood land, and gardens and keeping off grogeries."

"The discipline of the post is good," he reported, "arms and equipment in good serviceable order, and attention paid to the comforts of the men." He was much impressed with the small outlay of cash the army had made to build the Fort.

Colonel Mansfield thought that the population of Americans was at least 600 in the Humboldt Bay region but only 200 "capable of bearing arms in the four little towns on this bay." He saw pack trains departing almost daily from Union to the mining villages, and was much impressed with the growing lumber industry centered at Bucksport and Eureka. Except for beef, potatoes and barley he noted that "all other supplies came from San Francisco."[37]

So, the army was pleased with Fort Humboldt. The

[37]Frazer, *op. cit.*, pp. 119-20, 162-63 and 165. Distinguished-looking, white-bearded, old Major General Mansfield, after recapturing the infamous 40-acre Cornfield that bloody day at Antietam, was then killed.

unassuming Captain had done his part during his short tour, but he left the service, and the world rolled right along. Some Humboldt friends remembered soft-spoken Sam Grant as he headed for San Francisco and home, and later all would claim to have known him and to have been his friend. And Lt. Col. Buchanan continued to do his duty as he saw it.[38]

One of Grant's biographers believed that if Grant had not been so unhappy on Humboldt Bay he might have stayed in the army, become a senior quartermaster and ended his career, at best, as a colonel. Carrying on this line of reasoning, one could conclude that the Fort Humboldt days were directly responsible for saving the Union. This is too strong, but there is no doubt that Grant's hardships and attitudes formed on the West Coast helped make him the man he became. In any event, there was plenty of cause for Eureka and Humboldt County to celebrate "The Days of General Grant" and to reflect upon the area's significant effect on the course of our nation.

Given Grant's rise in the Civil War, and the jealousies and political background of the time, it is perhaps understandable that history has spotlighted the question of his drinking. What other criticism can be leveled at a painfully modest and quiet soldier, family-oriented, who sought no glory for himself nor manipulated the press to acquire high station.

In 1908, William C. Church, a former fellow-officer who knew him well, summed up:

There can be no doubt that General Grant did drink on

[38] Just before the Civil War, while still on the West Coast, Buchanan was the field commander in the Oregon "Rogue River War." Made a Brigadier General of Volunteers in 1862, he was breveted Major General (USA) in 1865. General Buchanan retired Jan. 1, 1871.

occasion, and we have good reason to believe, from personal observation, that most of the great soldiers of our Civil War drank at times something stronger than water...

The question, then, is not as to how much or little a soldier drinks, but whether he drinks at a time or in a way to impair his efficiency... General Grant did not drink on duty, and we have never yet met the man who could say of his own knowledge that he did so.[39]

M. Harrison Strong, the last surviving member of Grant's private staff in the Civil War, recorded his opinion in 1929.

For almost three years I was with General Grant at all hours of day and night. I never once saw him take a drink of whiskey and I never saw liquor of any kind either on his person or about his quarters.[40]

There is one more allegation about Grant's drinking that should be explored before bringing this chapter to a close. Lyle W. Dorsett, Professor of History at Wheaton College, Illinois, presented a paper on this subject at the April 1982, annual meeting of the Organization of American Historians and published a revised version in the fall of 1983.[41] In brief, Dr. Dorsett's thesis was that Grant was an alcoholic and that his alcoholism profoundly improved his generalship. His carefully constructed paper covered the usual historical sources but added new thoughts. Dorsett provided medical information on alcoholism which he believed fitted Grant's pattern of life. Dorsett wrote, "the wretched man was laden with guilt. No doubt his soul writhed in the pain of

[39] *Army/Navy Journal,* June 6, 1908.
[40] *Christian Science Monitor,* May 2, 1929. M. Harrison Strong, corporal-staff secretary.
[41] Lyle W. Dorsett, "The Problem of Ulysses S. Grant's Drinking During the Civil War," *Hayes Historical Journal,* Vol. IV, No. 2, Fall, 1983.

self-doubt and personal inferiority." He was a successful general suggests Dorsett, "because he had absolutely nothing to lose" and could smash on to victory.

Dorsett's thesis is not credible. Had a man with a loving wife and four dependent children nothing to lose? Did a soldier, admittedly modest, but brimful of optimism, calmly forging victory after victory, loathe himself? Perhaps Grant was a winning general because professionally he was a superb general. He knew, as Napoleon knew, that one never wins by relieving the pressure on the enemy.

Is it possible for any moderate social drinker to prove that he is *not* an alcoholic? It would be very difficult indeed if that person adopted the code of the Victorian gentleman which ruled that one should never seek publicity nor answer scandalous charges.

Grant was, as Dorsett wrote, a very private man who kept most of his feelings to himself or confided them only to his wife. His correspondence offered a few clues. "We are all well and me as sober as a deacon no matter what is said to the contrary."[42] If Grant was drunk in the Civil War, would not his political and military enemies have nailed him?

Dorsett comes very close to writing that those who drink heavily, if infrequently, and awaken with the tension of a hangover, are alcoholics. What specifically is meant by "alcoholism" must be defined. If it is not as a popular dictionary defines it, "a diseased condition resulting from the excessive or persistent use of alcoholic beverages," or an accepted medical definition, "The alcoholic is a person whose excessive use of alcohol results in serious medical, social, domestic, vocational, or

---

[42]U. S. Grant to Julia Dent Grant, Apr. 30, 1862.

legal problems," then what is it? Dorsett proves effectively that Grant did not meet these common definitions.

One contemporary expert believes that Dorsett strains at his arguments and, more important, seems to confuse drinking with alcoholism. If Grant were "truly an alcoholic, it probably would have ruined his Civil War career. Most telling is the argument that Grant's later drinking contradicts the consensus among alcohol specialists about the controversy over trying to condition alcoholics to drink socially."[43]

Grant did not resign his commission in California because he was an alcoholic, as Dorsett suggests. The controversial testimony of later years may spring from a need to appear as insiders with sensational information. Dorsett shows a woeful lack of appreciation for Grant's generalship and too much appreciation for historical mythology.

Dorsett suggests strongly that Lieut. Grant's early membership in the Sons of Temperance proves his alcoholism. On the contrary, it may have been an indication of enlightenment that alcohol is a powerful and debilitating stimulant. Does anyone allege that all of the church ladies active in the Womens Christian Temperance Union were alcoholics?

Dorsett also assumes that Grant inherited his weakness for liquor from his forebears. The thesis of inherited alcoholism, a most interesting one, has not been accepted universally. Grant knew the power of alcohol and thus insisted that he and his men not let it interfere with the performance of duty. A psychiatric study of why Grant led troops to victory in the West and in Virginia would,

---

[43] Letter from James E. Royce to the author, Mar. 7, 1986.

of necessity, require a more careful analysis than the simplistic conclusion Professor Dorsett has employed.

There are two characteristics that identify an alcoholic: an unreasonable urge to drink when one should not, and a craving or compulsion for the next drink. To an active alcoholic, both of these characteristics lead to an unmanageable life.

Dorsett makes too much of inherited tendencies even though they do exist. Recent studies show your chances of being an alcoholic double if your father was an alcoholic. Also Dorsett mistakenly equates the "Sons of Temperance" with Alcoholics Anonymous saying if Grant joined it was an acknowledgement of his alcoholism. In his article Dorsett reprints Grant's successor Rutherford B. Hayes' membership certificate in the "Sons of Temperance," but he does not say if Hayes was an alcoholic or had some other motive for joining.

The founders of Alcoholics Anonymous studied the failures of the nineteenth century movements in order to avoid similar failures. They found that the "Sons of Temperance," as well as a very popular later group called the "Washington Movement," had a fatal flaw. They did not require that its members admit to being alcoholic, and they did not exclude those who joined for other motives.

Of course, the later half of the nineteenth century was a hard drinking time. A loving wife might have put pressure on any husband, alcoholic or not, to stop drinking. And we know now that it is possible to be a heavy drinker and not an alcoholic.

Alcohol did not interfere with Grant's overall performance as a soldier or as a president. In his early life he was a hard drinker at most, rather than an alcoholic. The most important proof that Grant was not an alcoholic, however, is the evidence that he drank beer, wine or liquor, in moderate amounts, on occasions in later life. Someone who can function as a social drinker ought not to be labeled an alcoholic. The test for an alcoholic is not abstinence, it is moderation with alcohol in the system. Over the years, several misguided research professors have designed programs wherein recovered alcoholics could learn to drink again. Every one has concluded in grim and desperate tragedy.[44]

A federal panel recently investigated charges against two scientists, Drs. Mark and Linda Sobell, who believe alcoholics can be reformed into social drinkers. The panel found that the scientists' research contained "several errors" and was carelessly prepared. Dr. Mary Pendery charged, "the fact remains that the Sobells have not been able to come up with a single human being for whom the controlled drinking treatment worked."[45]

After studying and writing about Ulysses Grant for three decades Bruce Catton, America's most popular Civil War historian, ruminated about the myths that had become attached to Grant.

A number of historians, he reminisced, had developed a stereotyped picture of Grant that was inaccurate. He was often presented, thought Catton, as a heads-down slugger, a butcher who simply attacked and won solely because he had a larger army. "That is not a correct picture of Grant," he wrote. Catton believed Grant relied on nothing but swift movement and strategic insight.

Another myth that bothered Catton was the one that said Grant was a helpless drunkard. Catton believed that like most officers of all armies Grant would occasionally

---

[44]Letter from John C. Kavanagh to the writer, Sept. 8, 1984.
[45]*Seattle Times*, Sept. 13, 1984.

take a drink. But to go from there and say that he was a drunkard, guarded by his staff and bailed out of trouble, is "completely unjustified."

"All one needs to do," pointed out Catton, "is to reflect on two things. "He was always cold sober when the chips were down;" and even the times of his alleged benders, without exception, were times when nothing was happening and the General could be spared for a few days, if necessary.

But more than that, summarized Catton, Lincoln selected Grant, supported him, promoted him, and finally entrusted the entire war to him, on the ground that he was completely dependable. "And that," states Bruce Catton, "is the last characteristic you can ever find in an alcoholic."[46]

Catton's moving words on Grant's drinking are in his respected 1960 book, *Grant Moves South*.

> A man can get typed, justly or unjustly, and the shadow of the past, the dark stain of officers'-mess gossip, deposited over the years, can stay with him. Few of these men had actually known Sam Grant but in one way or another they had all heard of him: He was the officer who had had to resign his commission out West because he could not leave the bottle alone. Of the exact circumstances surrounding the resignation, of the loneliness and frustration that may have led man and bottle together, of the years of struggle that came thereafter, of the man's present determination to live down the past and make fullest use of his talents, of the hard core under the surface that would make his name terrible in war — of all these things the trim men in unweathered headquarters blue knew nothing. They knew only of the gossip, of the ineradicable stain, and that was enough.
>
> It would be enough for many others, then and thereafter, for the dark film left by gossip can never be entirely scrubbed

---

[46]Bruce Catton, *Reflections on the Civil War*, (New York, 1982), pp. 107-08.

away. In an army famous for the hard drinking done by men in shoulder straps, this was a handicap Grant would always have to carry. He began [the Civil War] as a colonel and he became a lieutenant general; by maneuvering and hard fighting he captured three rival armies entire; in four years he won command of all the troops in the United States, making himself the completely trusted instrument of the canniest judge of men who ever sat in the White House, enforcing unconditional surrender on dedicated men who had sworn to die rather than to submit; but the stain deposited by the gossip is still there, and men still cock their eyes and leer knowingly when Grant's name is mentioned; He drank. For men who do not know him, that has been enough.[47]

John Y. Simon summarized his conclusions in an article published in January 1974:

Old Army gossip ran that Grant had been drinking heavily on the Pacific Coast in the years 1852-1854, and that this had something to do with his resignation from the Army. Separation from his wife and children for years with no prospect of acquiring the money to reunite the family, recently promoted but not likely to rise again for many years, in poor health, assigned to a small and isolated post with a commanding officer he had disliked for years, Grant had plenty of reasons to resign, and documentary evidence proves that the resignation was his own choice. If, on the Pacific Coast, he drank more than was necessary . . . the evidence is too meager and contradictory for any sound conclusion.[48]

It seems clear that Grant was not a drunkard nor an alcoholic. Also, it seems clear that he drank off and on when he was on the Pacific Coast. The record is unclear that he drank much, or that he drank enough to impair his faculties or adversely affect his duties.

On one side we have the confusing testimony of

---

[47]Bruce Catton, *Grant Moves South*, (New York, 1960), pp. 38-39.

[48]John Y. Simon, "The Rediscovery of Ulysses S. Grant," *Inland: The Magazine of the Middle West*, Jan., 1974.

contemporaries, along with long-standing innuendos, rumor, and shady gossip. On the other side, in addition to other contemporary testimony, we have Grant's unvarnished record — a record that has stood the test of time and has stood scrutiny for generations.

In conclusion, what difference does it make? In the frontier army a non-drinker was a novelty. Grant entered the Civil War unimpaired; he probaby drank off and on at odd moments of that conflict, but entered the Presidency with no ill effects from liquor. There seems to be no question that hard liquors played no important part in the late years of his life.

But, we are stuck with the legend of Grant's drinking. Like the cherry tree and the dollar over the Rappahannock, it will stay with Americans forever.

Grant needs to be understood in the context of Humboldt Bay. Do periods of distress build character? Perhaps the answer is, "it depends." What happened on the Pacific Coast that helped to make Grant eventually a winner? How did Humboldt Bay influence what kind of a man Grant was to become?

We can only speculate that Grant became a better man because of his West Coast experiences. The enthusiasm he felt on going to California, his certainty that he could earn some extra money and bring his family West, his disappointment after seeing venture after venture melt away like the ice he sent to San Francisco, set him on a road where he had to pull himself up. His post-West Coast years were a time of further disappointments, but he survived. He survived with firmness of character, hard work, and loving support of his family. Those experiences molded him into the man he became. Frederick Jackson Turner, noted western historian, believed that the frontier experience shaped the American character. The writer believes that Grant's West Coast experience helped to develop his character for what lay ahead.

Allan Nevins reminds us:

> "He gained his place in... America... not by intellectual power, not by brilliance, cleverness or agile skill, and not by gifts of personality; he gained it by character."[49]

And the young captain, by his own choice, packed up at Fort Humboldt and headed towards San Francisco, his first step on the long way home to a joyful reunion with his family in Missouri and an uncertain economic future.

---

[49]Grant, *Papers*, Allan Nevins, "Preface," p. xix.

Chapter VII

"I Shall Be
On My Way Home"

On May 2, 1854, Grant wrote Julia his final letter from Fort Humboldt.[1] He told her to "discontinue writing" because he was going to wind up his affairs, both official and personal, and come home. The letter, full of discouragement, was written three weeks after he submitted his resignation and as he recovered from his second illness at Fort Humboldt. Grant wrote that on the "way I shall spend a week or ten days with John Dent" in Knight's Ferry.[2]

Grant left Humboldt Bay May 7th in Ryan, Duff & Co.'s steamer, the *Arispe* and during the trip he spent some time visiting with an older pioneer, W. I. Reed who was F. S. Duff's brother-in-law. The fellow passengers discussed horses and cattle in Humboldt County. Reed had a contract to supply Fort Humboldt with beef on the hoof and Grant spoke of his fondness for the horse "Eclipse." Later, Reed owned that horse and kept the

---

[1] The title of this chapter comes from U. S. Grant's May 2, 1854, letter to Julia Grant. Grant, *Papers*, p. 332.
[2] *Ibid.*

animal until it died of old age; many officers of the old army rode Eclipse and had nothing but praise for him. Reed told Grant that Eclipse was an Australian horse brought to California with about fifty others, all selected for their superiority.

Reed wrote later that he had been with Grant on several occasions and had an opportunity to observe him closely on the way to San Francisco. "Captain Grant was a striking example of rigid honesty and steadfastness of purpose."[3]

The *Arispe* under the command of Captain Pierce, had an uneventful trip and made good time to San Francisco — 27 hours — arriving on May 8. In addition to Grant and Reed there were eighteen other passengers, $25,000 in gold dust, and 70,000 board feet of lumber.[4]

When Grant arrived in San Francisco, he immediately called upon his friend Capt. T. H. Stevens, who was in the banking business. Grant had deposited $1,750 with Stevens in January 1854, (the going rate of interest was 2% a month) and wanted to take his funds home on the *Brother Jonathan* which was departing on May 16. Stevens could not produce the money, but he told Grant that if he would stay over until the *Sierra Nevada* sailed on June 1st he would have his money available.

Grant agreed reluctantly and went to visit Knight's Ferry. Returning to San Francisco the last day of May, Grant could not find Stevens who had conveniently found reasons to leave town.[5]

When Grant finally realized that Stevens was not going

[3]W. I. Reed to Col. William Conant Church, Aug. 25, 1909.

[4]*San Francisco Daily Alta California,* May 9, 1854.

[5]In 1863 Captain Thomas H. Stevens had still not paid his 1854 debt to Grant. Julia wrote him a stiff letter at that time demanding, and finally receiving, payment. Grant, *Papers,* p. 421.

to pay his debt, he went to the quartermaster's office in San Francisco to collect forty dollars in per diem pay which was owed to him by the government. His fellow townsman Brevet Major Robert Allen was then the quartermaster. As it was now late in the day, Allen had left the office. Richard L. Ogden, the office clerk, was about to close up when Grant presented his certificate for payment. Due to a clerical error in its preparation Ogden said that he could not cash it. Grant was distressed, told Ogden about his plans to sail the next day, and that he needed his funds for passage to New York.

Ogden, later an army Captain, told Grant he could sleep that night on a couch in Allen's office. The next morning Ogden reconsidered the certificate and cashed it. Ogden then told Grant that because of the volume of army business it was the practice of the steamship companies to transport army officers free. Ogden agreed to walk with Capt. Grant over to the steamship office and made arrangements for what was, except for meals and the Nicaraguan crossing, a free pass to New York.[6]

Stories written later that described Grant's arrival in San Francisco, impoverished and flat on his back, are false. In truth, Grant had several thousand dollars deposited and invested in San Francisco which he antici-pated would be the "nest egg" he would bring back to the states. James Grant Wilson wrote that Grant had "sums of money that were due him [in San Francisco], amount-ing to nearly three thousand dollars."[7] In those days of

[6]Colonel Nicholas Smith, *Grant, the Man of Mystery* (Milwaukee, 1909), pp. 51-53. Smith wrote that this account came from the journal of Captain Richard L. Ogden. Other accounts, more dramatic and adding to the story of Grant as a "down and outer," record that Major Allen introduced Grant to steamship officers who arranged for his passage to New York. Lewis, *op. cit.*, pp. 336-37; and Garland, *op. cit.*, pp. 128-29.

[7]James Grant Wilson, *General Grant* (New York, 1897), p. 77.

free wheeling, creative financing, and speculation, one debtor had vanished, another was short, and funds due from the army and Humboldt Bay had not yet arrived.

Again the man who had limitless confidence in his friends was let down by those same friends. Grant even wrote Stevens a friendly letter two weeks after Stevens failed him, asking Stevens to collect and distribute other funds to New York and Newport, Kentucky. This trusting trait would work to Grant's eternal disadvantage in the years to come.[8]

Normal sailing dates from San Francisco to Nicaragua were on the first and fifteenth of each month. With the establishment of a good-sized coaling station at San Juan del Sur, steamers could sail "non-stop" between San Francisco and Nicaragua. Average sailing time from San Francisco dropped to about twelve days, which approximated Grant's experience in the summer of 1854. After this, disciplined service was developed, the lake and river steamers could meet their schedules, and the Nicaragua crossing required only thirty-six hours. A year before Grant's trip, a record was set for passengers going to New York from San Francisco: twenty-two days and three hours.[9] Grant's trip, by comparison, took about twenty-four days.

Capt. Grant departed from San Francisco on June 1, 1854, on Vanderbilt's *Sierra Nevada,* one of 600 passengers. On June 13, the ship stood off San Juan del Sur, Nicaragua, and Grant recorded: "We have got this far safely and hope to tomorrow evening to get aboard of the

[8]U.S. Grant to Thomas H. Stevens, June 13, 1854. The author owns the original letter which was written on board the *Sierra Nevada* near San Juan del Sur, Nicaragua.

[9]Detail on the crossing from David I. Folkman, Jr., *The Nicaragua Route,* (Salt Lake City, 1972).

lake steamer. It's as hot as the final resting place of the wicked."[10]

San Juan del Sur was the Pacific gateway for Commodore Cornelius Vanderbilt's transit route across Nicaragua. In 1849, utilizing his experience as a Hudson River steamboat owner and operator, Vanderbilt pioneered an American route connecting San Francisco and New York City. The Nicaragua crossing involved negotiating the San Juan River and crossing Lake Nicaragua, as well as about seventeen miles of road between San Juan del Sur and the lake. When Vanderbilt's engineers reported that the San Juan River was not navigable, Vanderbilt took a small steamer up the river himself. To initiate the service, he used one large steamer on the lake and two smaller ones on the river.[11]

Several steamship lines transported passengers from San Francisco to Nicaragua, but Vanderbilt's Accessory Transit Company carried them across Nicaragua, and his Nicaragua Steamship line controlled the passage to New York. From San Juan del Sur, a road of about seventeen miles ran through the city of Rivas to the western lakeside village of San Jorge. In 1854 passengers on the narrow land-break rode in blue and white drawn carriages and stage coaches. At San Jorge travelers boarded a lake steamer which chugged 75 miles across Lake Nicaragua to San Carlos; then they utilized small boats to descend the San Juan River for about 100 miles to the Atlantic

[10]U.S. Grant to Thomas H. Stevens, June 13, 1854. On Oct. 23, 1879, while visiting Sacramento former President Grant was made a member of the Sacramento Society of California Pioneers, "an honor," he wrote, "which I highly prize." In signing the membership roll Grant wrote that he "Left S. F. in July, 1854, via Nicaragua." *West Coast Signal,* Nov. 5, 1879. Fountain Papers.

[11]N. S. B. Gras and Henrietta M. Larson, *Casebook in American Business History* (New York, 1939), p. 362.

port of San Juan del Norte, called Greytown by the British. From there, ocean steamers sailed directly to New York City.

The Panama Railroad was opened in 1855, and the Nicaragua route's traffic began to fall off. Political instability and disorder, filibustering, and the war with Costa Rica had more to do with closing the Nicaragua route than anything else.[12]

Captain Grant made the trip through Nicaragua without incident. Debarking at San Juan del Sur on June 14th he took the short stage to the edge of Lake Nicaragua, boarded the 120-ton lake steamer, transferred to a smaller river boat, and arrived at Point Arenas, just across the bay from San Juan del Norte.

Most travelers agreed that the nineteen-hour journey across Lake Nicaragua was the worst part of the crossing. The two lake steamers, *Central America* and *Ometepe,* had no food or sleeping accomodations. Decks became so crowded with stretched out bodies that it was difficult to walk around. But the trip on the San Juan River was no picnic either. Many times passengers could barely find standing room on one of the four crowded little steamers. Soot and cinders from the boat's funnel, combined with the humidity and rain showers, made travelers look like mud balls.

Ulysses Grant remembered the Isthmus crossing two years before and did not complain. He was going home and that was all that mattered. At Point Arenas, Grant saw the Transit Company workshops and houses; and it was here that workers assembled and maintained the small river steamers. "They [the steamers] all presented

[12]John Haskell Kemble to the author, Mar. 17, 1984.

quite a sight with their rusted chimneys, awnings flapping in tatters, and complete innocence of paint."[13]

On the San Juan del Norte side of the bay the old village had disappeared and new buildings were replacing them. The forest had been pushed back on all sides of the town, and streets, now in a pattern, had replaced the old and narrow foot paths. Several two-story wooden structures, brought down from the states in sections, served as hotels for tired travelers. Grant arrived at Greytown just in time to catch the three-decked, 1,207-ton steamer *Prometheus* which sailed for New York City on June 17, 1854. He had not a moment for rest in hotels or huts. It was close timing even by contemporary standards. The close coordination of trans-isthmian and ocean transportation was the aim of operators of the day. The Panama Railroad and steamers on either side of the Isthmus of Panama were operated so as to cut down the time between them to a minimum. Also, in Nicaragua the same standards were sought. *Prometheus* was instructed to wait until the steamboat had come down the San Juan River.[14]

Prometheus had a special niche in Vanderbilt's shipping empire. For one thing she was the only ship of that era ever ordered and paid for by an individual. Also, the steamboat that Vanderbilt personally took up the San Juan River was towed south to Nicaragua behind the *Prometheus*.

The year after Grant traveled the Nicaragua Route, thirty-two-year-old William Walker, leader of a filibuster army, took the town of Rivas, captured one of Vanderbilt's steamers on Lake Nicaragua, and in July 1856, was

---

[13]Folkman, *op. cit.*, p. 50.
[14]John Haskell Kemble to the author, Mar. 17, 1984.

inaugurated President of the Republic of Nicaragua. That planner of grandiose schemes died before a Honduran firing squad in September 1860, ending one of the most bizarre episodes of a Central America known for outrageous happenings.[15]

On June 25, 1854, *Prometheus* entered New York harbor, and Ulysses Grant was back in the "states." The *New-York Daily Times* of June 26 noted that the steamer carried "specie... 210 Cabin; 349 Steerage; total, 559" passengers. Listed among the cabin passengers were several army officers, including one "Capt. Grant, U.S.A." His fellow travelers included the French Consul's wife, the president of the Sacramento Railroad, three Van Rensselaer's, the Wells Fargo agent, and assorted gentlemen, ladies and children, and servants. Capt. Turner was the master.[16]

The first order of business for Capt. Grant was to collect money owed to him so that he could return to Julia in Missouri with cash to start his new life. Unfortunately, his experience of chasing elusive debtors in San Francisco was to be repeated. Grant decided to make a quick trip to Sackets Harbor to collect $800 which Elijah E. Camp owed him since June 1853. Grant notified Camp that he was coming and Camp left town. Grant returned to New York empty handed.

Julia's remembrance is that Ulys borrowed money from his friend Capt. Simon Bolivar Buckner to pay

---

[15]General description of Nicaragua's climate, geography and history comes from Allan Carpenter and Tom Balow, *Nicaragua* (Chicago, 1971); Henry I. Sheldon. *Notes on the Nicaragua Canal* (Chicago, 1902); and Harold Lavine, *Central America* (New York, 1964).

[16]*The New-York Daily Times*, June 26, 1854. The author is indebted to Dr. David L. Wilson, associate editor of the Ulysses S. Grant Association, for verifying Grant's arrival date in New York.

expenses to Sackets Harbor to chase Camp, and that Grant finally had to send home for money so that he could get to Missouri.[17]

Various accounts of Grant's arrival in New York, his financial straits, and his return home are similar. Most, as Albert D. Richardson and W. E. Woodward noted, had him shabby, broke, discouraged and embarrassed.[18] Lloyd Lewis reported him living on loans from fellow officers at Governor's Island, assisted by the future General Buckner, and finally rescued by a check from his father.[19] William S. McFeely called him "poor and forlorn" and hinted that Grant was afraid to return home not knowing what kind of a reception he would receive.[20]

Hamlin Garland wrote:

> He reached New York forlorn and practically penniless. He had just money enough to carry him to Watertown, where he hired a horse and rode to Sacket's Harbor. One of his recreant debtors lived there, and from him Grant expected to extract some money. He failed to obtain even an interview, and returned to New York in worse condition than ever.[21]

Years after the Civil War, Hamlin Garland interviewed General Buckner in Chicago. Garland's eight-page typescript note, "A Talk With General Buckner" was edited by Buckner who kept the original. In this interview Buckner agreed that Grant landed in New York poor and forlorn and came to his office to ask for help: "He had been staying at the old Astor House and his money was

---

[17] John Y. Simon., ed. *The Personal Memoirs of Julia Dent Grant* (New York, 1975), p. 72 and pp. 87-88 (cited hereafter as Julia Grant's Memoirs).

[18] Richardson, *op. cit.*, pp. 135-36. W. E. Woodward. *Meet General Grant* (New York, 1928), p. 121.

[19] Lewis, *op. cit.*, p. 338.

[20] William S. McFeely, *Grant: A Biography* (New York, 1981), pp. 56-57.

[21] Garland, *op. cit.*, p. 129.

gone... He asked for a loan in order to pay his bills at the hotel and reach his father in Southern Ohio."

Buckner knew the proprietor of the hotel and vouched for Grant who then "wrote on to his people in Southern Ohio and received money shortly after, enough to take him home." Buckner recalled that when the positions were reversed and "I became his prisoner Grant tendered me the use of his purse... it showed... his appreciation of my aid to him years before, which was really very little."[22]

Buckner took charge of Grant that summer of 1854 and in every way proved a true friend. When, after some days, the money arrived, Grant paid every dollar he owed in New York. Contrary to the many stories written on the subject, Buckner did not loan a cent to Grant. After the money from his father arrived, Grant resumed his journey to his old home in Ohio for a visit and then went on to join his wife and children in Missouri.[23] Within a matter of months, Buckner himself resigned from the army.

Because of later, more dramatic circumstances, the Grant-Buckner encounter interested every biographer of Grant and has been elevated to legendary status. John F. Hager writing in the Ashland, Kentucky *Daily Independent* reported, in "an entirely trustworthy account," that Capt. Buckner heard that Grant was in town, called upon him at the Astor House and assisted his friend with accommodation, meals, and money.[24] The next time the two friends met was when Buckner was forced into "unconditional surrender" by Grant at Fort Donelson.

[22]Garland Papers, "A Talk With General Buckner."

[23]Arndt M. Stickels, *Simon Bolivar Buckner* (Chapel Hill: The Univ. of North Carolina Press, 1940), p. 34.

[24]John F. Hager, *Ashland (Kentucky) Daily Independent*, Dec. 16, 1928. The Register of the Kentucky St. Hist. Soc. May, 1929.

After the war Buckner, who became Governor of Kentucky, remained a strong friend of Grant's and was an honorary pallbearer at Grant's funeral. Buckner died in 1914, one of the few Confederate generals who survived to that year.

The facts are, of course, that Grant had not heard from home and he was out of money. During his California absence he had regularly sent cash, negotiable paper and notes to Julia for her living expenses and their savings. Unable to collect what he had counted on, he had to write home: this was the money he awaited.

Leaving New York, bound for Cincinnati by rail, Grant stopped in Bethel, Ohio, about forty miles southeast of Cincinnati, to visit his mother and father. Jesse Grant thought his son had made a mistake in leaving the army and lost no time in telling him so. Grant's soft-spoken mother was, however, glad to see him out of the military. Perhaps she understood her son better, and the loneliness that he felt in army assignments. Gentle Hannah Grant was relieved to see Ulys return to civilian life and his family. Grant stayed with his parents about a week, regaining his health which had turned worse during the strenuous trip. With spirits now high, he said goodbye and began the last stage of his return trip by steamboat which would take him to St. Louis.

There is no record of the exact day that marked the return of Ulysses to the large white house on Gravois Creek. Grant himself remembered that it was "late summer." Wilson wrote that Grant "reached St. Louis late in August." Richardson hints the same, and McFeely voted for October.[25]

Frederick Dent Grant, the general's oldest son, and

---

[25]Grant, *Memoirs*, p. 219, Wilson, *op. cit.*, p. 78, Richardson, *op. cit.*, p. 136, McFeely, *op. cit.*, p. 56.

four years old at the time, recalled that his father returned in September 1854.

> I next remember seeing my father when he returned to my Grandfather Dent's house, near St. Louis . . . I was standing on the back porch of old White Haven when a man drew up near the back gate, in a buggy drawn by a white horse. One of the colored servants exclaimed, "La there's Mr. Grant!" In another moment my father sprang forward and took his two children in his arms.[26]

Lloyd Lewis captured that wonderful moment in writing of another eyewitness's reaction:

> . . . a slave girl, in the house, heard sounds of alarm on the long front porch where four-year old Freddie and his two-year old brother "Buck" were playing . . . The infants had taken fright at a dark-bearded man throwing the lap robe over the dashboard of a buggy at the front gate and climbing down.
>
> One look at the stranger, and the slave girl burst out through the door, past the whimpering children, and raced down the walk waving her arms and shrieking, "Fo de Law'ds sake! Hyar are Mars Grant!"[27]

Grant arrived home in Missouri in August 1854. This conclusion is based on his confirmed arrival date in New York, an estimate of his stay in New York City, his side trip to Sacket's Harbor, a week's visit with his parents in Ohio, and necessary travel time. Close dating of the White Haven arrival is not important. Grant's new beginning was.

This uncomplex young man, yearning to be a successful Missouri farmer, had seven years ahead of him before he reentered the army and began a steady march to Appomatox, the White House, and eternity. It is unquestioned that he became a great general and a great man. It is

---

[26]*Grant Association Newsletter* (Apr., 1969), p. 18.
[27]Lewis, *op. cit.*, p. 339. Julia's sister Emmy is the source.

unfortunate, and perhaps predictable, that he was not a great president. Many Grant biographers depict those seven years as poverty stricken, spirit breaking, and even liquor dominated.

It is true that after his return from California, and before he trudged off to war from Galena, he and his growing family went through a hard scrabble. The whole country experienced hard times. For many reasons he did not succeed in farming. His short attempt as a rental agent in St. Louis was disastrous, and his acceptance of a stingy father's largess was hard to swallow. But Ulysses Grant's transitional years were generally happy, peaceful, and hardworking ones.

The young Grants had servants, lived in comfortable homes, and had a normal family life that befitted their social and professional station. Even the highly publicized log cabin that Grant built, while rough and hand hewn, was comfortably furnished and cozy. The family lived there "scarcely three months."[28] Before moving to the two-story log house in 1856, Ulysses and Julia occupied Wish-ton-wish, "a beautiful English villa... situated in a primeval forest of magnificent oaks." This house belonged to Julia's brother, Lewis Dent who had returned to California.[29] When Julia's mother died, and her lonely father insisted, the Grants moved back into beautiful White Haven with its stables, barns, and slave quarters. When the Grants went into St. Louis, where Ulysses entered into partnership with Harry Boggs, they secured a neat little house with drawing room and a garden with peach and apple trees. They took four servants with them.[30]

[28] Julia Grant Memoirs, p. 79.
[29] Ibid., p. 78.   [30] Ibid., p. 80.

At Galena, Grant rented a seven-room brick house which was nestled high on a hill in the best neighborhood and with a lovely view. Julia had a maid since the family decided not to take the slaves along to northern Illinois.[31]

And although it is perfectly proper to call Ulysses Grant a clerk in a leathergoods store, he was there, as his brothers before him, to learn the trade, expand their wealthy father's business, and become a partner. The record shows that he was on that track when an incident far away in Charleston, South Carolina changed America forever.

Grant's life between 1855 and 1861 was essentially a continuation of his frontier beginnings; he was always the westerner, moving, trying to better himself, and working hard. At West Point, in Panama, at Hardscrabble, he knew instinctively that the way to get something done was to get on with it. And that is how he did his job in the Civil War. Grant took the resources at hand and got on with the work. Even Lincoln, a westerner himself, was amazed that Grant did not ask for more time, more horses, more cannon, or whatever. Grant just got on with the job. Not everything he attempted in his post-Pacific years was successful, but everything he did was based on common sense, high morals, and an optimistic outlook.

In the late summer of 1854, young Sam Grant did not know what lay ahead, but he undertook the job of making a living, raising his family, and being a respected citizen of his community. He had survived his trial on the West Coast and was a better man for it.

Grant wanted always to return to California. In his twilight years he wrote:

[31] *Ibid.*, p. 84.

I left the Pacific coast very much attached to it, and with the full expectation of making it my future home. That expectation and that hope remained uppermost in my mind until the Lieutenant-Generalcy bill was introduced into Congress in the winter of 1863-4. The passage of that bill, and my promotion, blasted my last hope of ever becoming a citizen of the further West.[32]

I spent two years there in early life, and always felt the greatest desire to make it my future home. Nothing ever fell over me like a wet blanket so much as my promotion... As junior major-general in the regular army I thought my chances good for being placed in command of the Pacific division when the war closed. As lieutenant-general all hope of that kind vanished.[33]

The years between his Pacific Coast experience and the Civil War were years of difficulty, but they were years of preparation for Ulysses Grant. Hard outdoor labor strengthened his body. The love and close family circle that he enjoyed nurtured his soul. His thoughtful contemplation of national events educated him and all the while, unknown to himself, he was being prepared for another trial, so important that a nation was at stake.

Grant had time to ponder at how the world was organized, how his sense of values matched up to that world around him. Was his country headed for an inevitable conflict? Would the South secede if a Republican was elected? What was the impact of the great West which he had seen at first hand? How would the growth of that huge land change the America that had been guided by a handful of Eastern states for so long?

In many careers, men have experienced a kind of forced

[32]Grant, *Memoirs*, p. 210.
[33]U. S. Grant to Elihu B. Washburne. *General Grant's Letters to a Friend.* (New York, 1897).

idleness, during which they thought and grew toward what would be their greatest contribution. Lincoln did so between his terms in Congress and the presidency, and Washington between the French and Indian War and the Revolution. Churchill had his fallow years in the 1930s; DeGaulle withdrew to his farm before his last service in government, and Eisenhower languished sixteen years as an over-qualified major. Ulysses Grant's seven years served the same noble purpose.

By 1886, one year after Grant died, his Fort Humboldt cottage had fallen apart. The walls had been stripped of plaster, the doors were off the hinges, the windows were smashed, and the sagging roof was almost completely gone. The rear of the little house was almost buried in a mass of climbing vines.[34] But the spirit of the young captain who paced the grounds there can still be felt by visitors on that windswept hill.

Ultimately any final verdict on U. S. Grant must be judged on the bedrock of his own strength of character — and it was imperishable.

_____

[34]N. S. Giberson, "Captain Grant's Old Post, Fort Humboldt." *The Overland Monthly*, Vol. VIII-Second Series, 1886, p. 136.

U.S. Grant, age 57, in San Francisco, California.
Portrait by I.W. Taber.
Courtesy, California Historical Society, San Francisco.

Epilogue

The Return of Ulysses

Despite some disappointments, lost opportunities, and lonely circumstances, Ulysses Grant was favorably impressed with the Pacific Coast and until late in the Civil War planned to make it his civilian home. He told a journalist friend in 1879 that "it had always been the dream of my life to live in California."[1] Return he did to the West Coast, but it was only for visiting and sightseeing during his later years.

After circling the globe Ulysses and Julia Grant, with their accompanying party, arrived in San Francisco on September 20, 1879. They had been gone from the United States for about two and one-half years. They had seen sights and received welcomes that were almost indescribable.

The former President had been given the freedom of London, dined with Queen Victoria, met with Prince Bismarck in Germany, the Czar in Russia, the Pope, the King of Spain, the Sultan of Turkey, the ruler of Egypt,

[1] John Russell Young, *Around the World With General Grant* (New York, 1879), Vol. II, p. 628.

the King of Siam, and the Chinese Prince Regent and Viceroy, among other distinguished personages. He was enthusiastically received from Edinburgh, to India, and throughout the Orient. It was a triumphal tour truly like none other in American history.

It is possible that when Grant was welcomed by thousands of San Franciscans at the close of this world voyage his fame was at an all-time high. The greatest soldier of his time, although a mediocre president, still was considered by most Americans to be the same honest hero of Appomatox, untouched by the scandals of his administration. His return to the West Coast was indeed a high water-mark of his life.[2] Grant was surprised when he learned from newspapers delivered by the pilot boat of the magnitude of the welcome, the enthusiasm, and the honors that San Francisco had planned.

John Russell Young, who accompanied Grant around the world, recalled that the sun was setting that Saturday evening as the *City of Tokio* steamed through the Golden Gate. He thought the scene and the sounds wonderously impressive, framed by brown hills, serenaded by fog-horns, paced by yachts and steamers bright with flags, and thrilled by the cheers from thousands of well-wishers on Telegraph Hill. The thundering batteries on Angel Island and Fort Mason (then Black Point) continued their roll as the ship glided toward its anchorage at the foot of a city blazing with brilliant lights.

The *City of Tokio* was one of the Pacific Mail's newest ships: She had screw-propellers rather than paddles. The reception committee went out to meet Grant's ship and so did Major General Irvin McDowell and his staff aboard a

---

[2] Jerome A. Hart, *In Our Second Century* (San Francisco, 1931), p. 302. Also, *General Grant Abroad* (Chicago, 1879), p. 286.

government steamer. When the *Tokio* stopped, the first person to greet the Grants was their son, Ulysses, Jr., who clambered aboard. Next came Grant's old classmate, "a large, almost burly man, of imposing appearance."[3] "How are you, Mac?" said Ulysses as they shook hands. McDowell, as head of the Military Department of the Pacific, had the job Grant thought he wanted when the Civil War was over.

Although the high-ranking welcoming committee had decided to have the official reception on Monday because of the weekend arrival, the people decided otherwise. Crowds had been waiting all day on hills and rooftops, and nighttime or not, the celebration began. Clearly General Grant was the idol of the people and the man of the hour.

Cannon continued to boom, whistles screeched, church bells rang, brass bands played, and bonfires were lit as the Grants drove in a carriage through vast throngs of cheering people. Deafened by cannon and blinded by smoke the arriving party could hardly see a thing. As the procession moved through the city "Johnnie Comes Marching Home" was sung over and over again by the crowds. One observer noted that, by request, the general was high on the carriage box where he could be viewed more easily. "The silent Grant made his way, ever bearing the same impassive face, with just a faint suspicion of a smile."[4]

It was almost midnight when the Grants reached their luxurious suite at the world famous Palace Hotel on Market Street. Opened in 1875, the original Palace was

---

[3]Robert J. Chandler, "The Press and Civil Liberties in California During the Civil War" (Ph.D. dissertation, Univ. of California, Riverside, 1978), p. 307.

[4]Hart, *op. cit.*, p. 295.

destroyed later by the earthquake and fire of 1906. Built when Nevada's fabulously rich silver mines poured millions of dollars into San Francisco each month, the Palace was a symbol of the color and verve of the bonanza period. Grant, Sherman, Sheridan, and every other important visitor stayed at the Palace. The hotel's Grand Court was roofed in glass, encircled by layers of balconies rising above a garden of lemon, orange, and lime trees. "It was at least four times too big for its time and place," Oscar Lewis noted, "but then San Francisco never had a sense of proportion."[5]

Grant's initial public remarks expressed "his heartfelt pleasure at being once more in California, after twenty-five years' absence." Hamlin Garland wrote that Grant retained "a most singular affection for Humboldt Bay and Fort Vancouver.... One of his first expressions was: 'I want to go to Oregon, to the old fort.'"[6]

The next day, which was beautiful even by California standards, committees, delegations, and officers called upon the general at his hotel. Major General McDowell hosted a "sumptuous dinner" at Fort Mason, followed by a large reception. Everybody of importance was invited, and Julia noted "no country I had seen could have assembled a more distinguished-looking or handsomer company."[7]

Wealthy Mr. and Mrs. Charles Crocker had a reception at their huge and new residence on Nob Hill. Five hundred of San Francisco's society came. Senator Wil-

[5]Oscar Lewis and Carroll D. Hall, *Bonanza Inn: America's First Luxury Hotel* (San Francisco).

[6]Hamlin Garland, *Ulysses S. Grant: His Life and Character* (New York: 1920), pp. 470-71.

[7]John Y. Simon, ed., *The Personal Memoirs of Julia Dent Grant* (New York, 1975), p. 308.

liam Sharon, the lumber and rail baron, gave a splendid ball at his country place in Belmont. One thousand guests arrived in special trains. The Grants stayed overnight and Julia reported cheerfully that "the wine flowed like water."[8] Hardly the remark of a wife worried about an alcoholic husband. Breakfast was with the James C. Floods, former barkeep now millionaire, at Menlo Park, and former Governor Leland Stanford had the Grants spend a day at his farm in Palo Alto. Dinner was at Millbrae where the home of Mr. and Mrs. Darius O. Mills, another Comstock millionaire, was illuminated like a fairyland, with table appointments and decorations excelling anything the visitors had seen yet. The Grants had now said farewell to the middle class and were at ease with the very rich for the remainder of their lives.

Campfires, fancy balls, army meetings, and parades almost wore out the famous couple as the days went by. But Grant kept pace with the rapidly changing hosts and hostesses. Most of all, he enjoyed seeing individuals he had known during earlier West Coast days. Dr. Jonathan Clark from Humboldt Bay made a special trip to San Francisco to see his former friend and patient. Grant was surrounded by a throng of callers in the Palace's drawing room when he spotted Clark. The former president immediately moved over and greeted Clark with cordial words asking about many of the people he remembered from Eureka. Dr. Clark reported later that "Grant had nothing but the kindest words" for his former Humboldt companions and "regarded them with the same quiet kindliness with which he held them in the dark days of his residence at the dreary western garrison."[9]

[8] *Ibid.*
[9] Shield's Article.

Grant's genuine pleasure and good will toward his final West Coast post is another piece of evidence that contradicts old army gossip about Fort Humboldt. John Russell Young, Grant's newspaper friend, was surprised at the number of old companions who turned up in San Francisco and at their mutual congeniality with the general.[10]

There were more visits to City Hall, stock exchanges and banks, reviews of Civil War veterans, and a private meeting with members of the Methodist Conference, who paid a call in a body. Grant handled one potential problem with his usual calm and forthright manner.

At Maj. General McDowell's home at Fort Mason the delicate question of whether or not Grant should receive a delegation from the Chinese community of San Francisco was debated. Since the Chinese were not well liked by the white citizenry there were some objections for fear that it would give offense to the people of California. But Grant had never any faith in McDowell's judgment as a diplomat nor a politician. He wrote Secretary Edwin M. Stanton during the Civil War that "McDowell is only a soldier and has never been anything else . . . [and] is likely to do more harm than good" [in California].[11]

When Grant thought the Chinese matter over, he noted characteristically that he had been received with kindness and respect by the statesmen and rulers of that country and therefore he would be very happy to respond by any courtesy he could show the Chinese in America. Thus the potentially troublesome episode became a happy event of cordial exchanges between Ulysses and Julia and the admiring Chinese merchants.[12]

[10] Young, *op. cit.*, pp. 628-29.
[11] *Official Records*, Vol. 50, pt. 2, p. 945.
[12] Young, *op. cit.*, pp. 586 and 592.

The friendliness of San Francisco affected Grant deeply. His face showed an appreciation of the spontaneous outpouring of affection and his natural, quiet nature was overcome. He talked freely and entered into the spirit of the occasion in a grand and open manner. When the mayor suggested that Grant did not have to shake hands with hundreds of formal callers, the general reached back in his memory and said he could "fight it out on that line."[13] On one occasion Grant corrected publicly the reported dates of his earlier Western visits. "This is to show, in a quiet way, that the charges made against him... of dissolute habits, while residing there, were wholly false, as the year given... was before he had ever seen the place."[14]

One delightful side trip took the Grants to Yosemite where the general made a deep and favorable impression on Alfred, one of the best known Sierra "whips," who drove many illustrious visitors on the daily stage between Wawona and the gorgeous Yosemite Valley. One of the Yosemite Commissioners talked with the famous stage driver after Grant's trip:

> He said to me that he had never permitted but one man to take the reins from him in his life, and that was President Grant. The general drove nearly all the way to Inspiration Point, said Alfred, and lighted at least four cigars. He took in everything along the road, and made all the turns as perfectly as an old driver.[15]

Grant's party were enthralled with long drives through the Sierra, nights spent in out-of-the-way inns, and the hearty welcome expressed by the inhabitants of small

[13]J. T. Headley, *The Travels of General Grant* (Philadelphia, 1881), p. 586.
[14]*Ibid.*, p. 599.
[15]*San Francisco Examiner*, May 24, 1892, in Richard N. Scheller's Papers, p. 309, Calif. Hist. Soc. Lby.

wayside towns. The general in high spirits climbed, rode over the peaks, and enjoyed the freedom and movement of the outdoor life. The entire party agreed that Yosemite Valley was the most impressive sight they had seen during the entire trip.[16]

Typical Western openness and humor followed Grant.

"Stand in the light, general, where we can see you," one mountain man shouted. "But I look better in the dark," replied Grant. "We'll make you President [again]," was shouted often. "I was a Confederate soldier . . . but God bless your old soul," yelled another. "General, since you came to the coast business is better, money is flowing, and people are happier," an enthusiastic politician noted. Grant said, "I guess wheat going up thirty cents a cental has more to do with it than I have."[17]

After enjoying the beauty of Yosemite the Grants moved on to Stockton. They were met at the highly decorated railway station by a cheering crowd, a band, military units, and all the dignitaries of Stockton. Schools were dismissed for the day so the children could gather at Hunter Street Square hoping to see Grant as he went to a large banquet in his honor at the new Yo Semite House. When Grant saw the children he "descended from his carriage and reviewed the little people to their great delight."[18]

Julia found herself surprised by the sternness of her husband's remarks at the banquet. He spoke directly and earnestly about how it was impossible for him to have done all the visiting, camping, and mining alleged to him

---

[16]Young, *op. cit.*, p. 631.

[17]Garland, *op. cit.*, p. 472.

[18]*Stockton Daily Independent*, Oct. 1, 1879, in Ronald Rayman's article "Stockton's Yo Semite House: 1869-1923," p. 168, Calif. Hist. Qtly., Sept. 1977.

in the 1850s since he had never been in Stockton for more than one hour before in his life.[19] Grant was striking back indirectly at the whiskey legends which had grown up around his West Coast tenure. He had heard enough.

In mid-October the Grants sailed up to Oregon and Washington through rough seas but with companionable fellow travelers. Greeted by the territorial governor, the army's commander of the Columbia Department, and members of the legislature, Ulysses and Julia passed between hundreds of Vancouver citizens holding blazing torches as they departed their steamer for a memorable reception. Bonfires were lit all over the city, Chinese paper lanterns gave the occasion a festive air, and all the big homes were decorated and lighted along the parade route.

During the formal ceremonies Washington's Governor Elisha P. Ferry made a fervent plea for statehood which came as a surprise to Grant. Grant admitted to the crowd that he had not yet visualized Washington Territory as a candidate for statehood, but after this visit he was convinced it must come soon. Soon took another ten years.

Grant saw many of his old army friends while in the Pacific Northwest and the party was entertained with cordial hospitality. He was especially animated and enthusiastic as he introduced Julia to the people and the country that remained so bright in his memory. Grant took special pleasure in showing Julia Fort Vancouver, the old "quartermaster's ranch" (protected then by a substantial fence), and his famous potato patch. They rode up the Columbia toward The Dalles and Julia agreed

---

[19] Julia Dent *Memoirs, op. cit.,* p. 309.

with her husband that the beautiful scenery, the broad river, and towering Mount Hood were indeed outstanding.

In Portland, at an enthusiastic reception, Grant responded to the honors given him at some length, and talked about his prior residence and acquaintances on the Pacific Coast. Grant was proud of his early days in the West and gave no sign of any embarrassing circumstances connected with that period.[20]

The Grants moved on to Sacramento where they were astounded at the beauty of the private residences there. After sightseeing, a reception, and dinner, Julia was delighted when a black woman came forward with hand outstretched. "Miss Julia," she said, "I do not believe you know me. I am Henrietta, or Henny, as you used to call me at home." Julia took both her hands, told her how glad she was to see her, and recalled that Henny had been one of the Dent's household slaves. Old Col. Dent had sent Henny to California with George Dent to look after the children when the younger Dent moved to Knight's Ferry nearly a quarter century before.[21]

When he spoke to the Society of Pioneers in Sacramento Grant recalled his life on the Pacific Coast as "a pleasant one." He said that he had formed many attachments for the country, and the people, and never abandoned the hope of making his permanent home in California. During his years in Missouri as a farmer, Grant said that he had thought constantly of returning, but had never been able to do so; and then in 1861, he remarked dryly, "other events had intervened."[22]

[20]L. T. Remlap, pseud. L. T. Palmer, *General U. S. Grant, His Life and Public Services* (Chicago, 1885), p. 586.

[21]Julia Dent *Memoirs, op. cit.*, p. 311.

[22]Garland, *op. cit.*, p. 471.

Upon leaving San Francisco to return East, thousands of men formed lines with lighted torches singing "He's a Jolly Good Fellow." The Grants went to Lake Tahoe, on to Virginia City and Carson City, Nevada, Cheyenne, and Omaha. They tarried as they headed back to Galena and then on to Chicago and to their original starting point, Philadelphia. The long journey was over.

Later, Julia wrote in her own Victorian style:

> It would take a volume or a poet to tell all one feels when one first visits our beautiful Far West. The magnificent, the infinite sweep of plain; the majesty, the magnitude of the mountains; the very forests here are heroic in their grandeur; and the Pacific — one must fall prostrate on first beholding its majestic grandeur.[23]

Mrs. Grant finally understood how young Captain Grant felt when he first saw those sights and wrote her that he saw their future on the Pacific Coast.

Four years later, in the fall of 1883, Henry Villard, German-born president of the Northern Pacific Railroad, gathered a distinguished company in Chicago to travel with him in special cars to the newly-established western terminus of the Northern Pacific in Tacoma, Washington Territory.

Villard's invitation came at a time U. S. Grant was facing a perplexing problem that has bothered many of our former presidents. How does one spend his time after leaving the White House? Grant was tied into Mexican railroad adventures with Jay Gould, and was to become a disgraced dabbler in Wall Street affairs. In accepting Villard's invitation Grant may have made himself a party to a promotion beneath the dignity of a former chief executive.

---

[23]Julia Dent *Memoirs, op. cit.,* p. 310.

In addition to the former President, eastern American travelers included the Secretary of the Interior, the Attorney General, several Governors, Congressmen, and business leaders Jay Cooke, George M. Pullman, J. S. Pillsbury and Marshall Field. There were assorted generals, railroad and bank presidents, big city and small town mayors, and judges.

An impressive gathering of foreigners went along with Villard, a promoter of the first rank: The British Minister Plenipotentiary, and Imperial German Minister, at least three counts from Austria-Hungary, Denmark, Sweden and Norway, a baron or two, earls, the Governor of the Bank of England, and the Lord Chief Justice of England.

And from the West Coast came a group of dignitaries to enjoy Villard's hospitality and the ride home. Included in this number were San Francisco, Portland, Sacramento, and Walla Walla businessmen and elected officials. Chamber of Commerce and Board of Trade presidents, Oregon's Secretary of State, consular officers representing their countries on the West Coast, and Noah Shakespeare, the Mayor of Victoria, British Columbia, joined the party.

The group was well-received by the public wherever it appeared — Minneapolis, St. Paul, Bismarck, Billings, rail sidings, and on to the coastal cities.

Usually when General Grant stepped up to specially constructed platforms there would be a tremendous roar from crowds that had been waiting sometimes for hours. A writer on the scene called the shouts "terrifying" as the people tried to show their affection for the victorious general. He noted that the common people of America loved Grant as the man who saved the union and honored him as a brave soldier.

At one stop along the way an observer recorded that Grant sat grim and silent as young girls showered his carriages with flowers. He wore a white plug hat and gripped the stubby remains of a cigar that he had been smoking. A conclusion from one listener was that "Grant was no public speaker," and although he had a sense of humor, his voice seemed weak.

Along the route, crowds would demand a speech from Grant. In Bismarck he shared the platform with Sitting Bull, once the terror of Dakota. Grant would usually comply with a few remarks of courtesy, but whenever possible he would slip away. One description of the general in 1883 recorded that except for the fire in his eyes, and the stern set of his mouth, there was little to remind the public of Grant the soldier. "He became quite rotund and now has a red face; he looks more like a corpulent craftsman than a general or president."[24]

Arriving in Portland, Oregon, early in September 1883, Villard's party "inspected" Portland and its vicinity, went to Astoria, Kalama, and later on to Tacoma, Victoria, British Columbia, and Seattle, Washington Territory.

Thursday night, September 13, Villard, his guests, and the "elite" of Portland accepted an invitation extended by the Chinese merchants of the city to attend a performance at the Hong-Low Theater. The theater had been newly decorated for the occasion with "gorgeous curtains... and new and handsome coverings." Regular theater goers were turned away as "new and rich wardrobe[s]... were used for the first time and the actors presented a brilliant appearance.[25]

---

[24]Nicolaus Mohr, *Excursion Through America* (Chicago, 1973), p. 201. This edition edited by Ray Allen Billington.

[25]*The Daily Post Intelligencer*, Seattle, Wash. Terr., Sept. 14, 1883.

The local drama critic reported that the performance was a mixture of "opera, japollay, tumbling, etc.," that the audience applauded liberally, and the guests were delighted. The cymbal player was given special mention. When he exerted himself many of the audience clapped their hands over their ears. The writer admitted that "to many of our foreign visitors it will be one of the strangest scenes witnessed in their travels."[26] It does not take much imagination to visualize tone-deaf Ulysses Grant cringing inwardly with those strange sounds, bangs and clatter. It must have been painful for the old warrior.

Both Portland and Seattle worked hard to entertain the distinguished visitors. Decorated and temporary viewing stands were filled, with bands playing and crowds cheering. Big parades were held in both cities. Seattle had its largest barbeque in history, and Portland featured an outdoor concert by the 21st U. S. Infantry Regimental Band. "The charming young women of the country, clothed in their finest evening dress made an excellent impression" on the visitors.[27] After a side trip to Victoria, B. C., and a boat trip up to The Dalles, the party headed for Yellowstone Park and back to Chicago recalling vividly their week on the coast.

The former President did not appear to be at his best during his trip with the Villard party. Quieter than usual, less stirred by the crowds who called for him, his remarks became shorter and less spontaneous as the trip progressed. Grant did not feel well, but he made no complaint nor mentioned his health to anyone.

The old general returned to his home in New York City on September 21. He was surprised that the trip over

[26] Ibid.
[27] Mohr, op. cit., p. 201.

Northern Pacific rails had shown him such a rich and rapidly developing country. Grant thought that this expedition just about completed his personal observations of every section of America. And he was pleased with what he saw: "Across its continent where but a few years ago the Indian held undisputed sway, there is now a continuous settlement . . . "[28]

Grant was tired upon his return. He wrote to his niece that he and Julia would probably never visit Europe again. "We are getting a little too old to enjoy traveling," he wrote her.[29]

Eight months after returning, on June 2, 1884, Grant took a bite from a peach after his noontime dinner and jumped up immediately from the table in pain. Julia thought he had been stung by an insect but the momentary, almost unbelievable pain was evidently the first indication of the malignant throat cancer that would kill Ulysses Grant.

The next summer a bundled-up Grant slumped on a cottage porch at the Mount McGregor, New York, resort. He was fighting to stay alive to finish his book which was to bring financial security to his beloved Julia. As he applied his great talent of massive concentration to his final task on earth, Grant paused on occasion to look out at the mountain slope and the trees. His thoughts may have strayed to youthful days and ancient redwoods on the Pacific Coast which remained high in his affection.

On July 23, 1885, Grant died. The bravest of the brave, and a citizen as true to his country's best hopes as any other American, was gone. Mark Twain wrote that

---

[28]Jesse Grant Cramer, ed., *Letters of Ulysses S. Grant* (New York, 1912), p. 154.
[29]*Ibid.* p. 155.

Grant's *Memoirs* will "bring to American ears, as long as America shall last, the roll of his vanished drums and the tread of his marching hosts."[30]

Although it should ever be so, it may not have turned out that way. The trial of U. S. Grant was over in 1885, and yet one hundred years later many Americans are uncertain still as to the verdict.

---

[30]John Y. Simon, ed., *General Grant by Matthew Arnold with a Rejoinder by Mark Twain* (Carbondale, Ill. 1966), p. 57.

Chronology

1852

July 5   U. S. 4th Infantry regiment departs in the *Ohio* from New York Harbor for Panama.

July 16   *Ohio* arrives at the port of Aspinwall in Navy Bay, Panama.

July 17   4th Infantry debarks from the *Ohio*, takes railroad to Barbacoas, boards native canoes, and starts up the Chagres River.

July 20   Lt. Col. Bonneville, with main body of troops, arrives in Panama City and boards the *Golden Gate*.

July 21   Cholera breaks out on the *Golden Gate*. U. S. Grant, still on the trail, signs contract for mules to move his party to Panama City.

July 22   U. S. Grant, Jr., born in Bethel, Ohio.

July 28   Captain Grant purchases 249 blankets in Panama City.

August 1   U. S. Grant is aboard the *Golden Gate* in Panama Bay near Taboga. Major Gore dies.

August 5   *Golden Gate* sails from Panama to California.

August 9   *Golden Gate* near Acapulco, Mexico.

August 16   *Golden Gate* at San Diego, California, in the morning, proceeding northward towards San Francisco.

August 18   *Golden Gate* arrives at San Francisco harbor after standing offshore waiting for the fog to lift. She made a fast trip of 11 days, 21 hours.

August 20   Grant having arrived moves in with his old classmate

Capt. Frederick Steele, writes his first letter from Benicia, California.

August 21   Aboard the *Sophie* Grant makes his first trip to interior California to visit his in-laws, the Dent brothers.

August 29   Grant reluctantly ends his visit in Knight's Ferry and heads back to Benicia.

August 31-September 2   Capt. Grant spends a few days in San Francisco and is very impressed.

September 4   Capt. Grant reports to an official "Board of Survey" investigating losses of public property in Panama. The Board found no fault with Grant's performance.

Week of September 5   Each day Ulysses rides out from Benicia to the neighboring communities, visiting among others, Vallejo, the State Capital.

September 14   Grant departs San Francisco Bay in the *Columbia* bound for Oregon Territory.

September 20   The 4th Infantry arrives at its new post on the Columbia River.

Early October   Grant travels to Fort Dalles, upriver from Columbia Barracks.

December   Ulysses writes Julia that he loves the West and hopes the family can join him.

1853

January   Grant and Ingals are the first of the season to walk across the frozen Columbia River.

February 15   Ulysses hints to Julia that he may be transferred to Fort Humboldt, a less desirable post with no family quarters.

March 21   Grant plowing and planting his potatoes. He reports that he has grown a sizeable beard.

April   Grant busy doing quartermaster reports, property accounts, and subsistence papers.

May 15-June 14   Capt. Grant, on temporary assignment from Columbia Barracks, is in California.

July 31   Grant uses the name "Columbia Barracks" for the final time in official reports; the post is called Fort Vancouver the next month.

August Unknown to Grant, his commission as regular army captain becomes effective.

September Capt. Grant requests temporary assignment to Washington D.C. to settle quartermaster accounts and visit his family.

September 24 Grant departs for San Francisco on official business.

October 12 From San Francisco Capt. Grant writes Washington officials attempting to get to Washington D.C.

October 30 He returns to Fort Vancouver.

November 26 Grant reports on his dealings with Peter Skene Ogden, chief factor of the Hudson's Bay Company.

December Grant spends his second Christmas away from Julia.

1854

January 3 U. S. Grant, having been transferred from Fort Vancouver, departs from San Francisco in the *John S. McKim* bound for Humboldt Bay.

January 5 Grant reports in at Fort Humboldt.

January 18 First letter to Julia from Fort Humboldt.

February 2 "Nobody knows how forsaken I feel here," Grant expresses his loneliness.

February 5 Grant has a tooth pulled.

February 18 and 20 Lt. Col. Buchanan assigns Grant to two routine "Boards of Survey."

February 28 U. S. Grant recorded as "sick" on Fort Humboldt official rolls.

March 25 Letter to Julia shows Captain Grant desperately discouraged with his situation.

April 11 Grant receives his formal commission as Captain. He writes his acceptance and his resignation from U. S. Army.

April 27 U. S. Grant 32 years old.

April 30 Grant recorded as "sick" on Fort Humboldt official rolls.

May 1 Lt. Col. Buchanan writes that Grant is "too sick to travel."

May 2 Letter to Julia; "I am coming home in 4-6 weeks, will go by Knight's Ferry."

May 3 Routine reports completed.

May 7 Grant departs from Humboldt Bay in the Steamer *Arispe*.

May 8   Ulysses Grant arrives in San Francisco.

Mid-May   He is in Knight's Ferry visiting his brothers-in-law.

May 31   Grant arrives back in San Francisco.

June 1   He departs from San Francisco on the way home.

June 2   In Washington, D. C. Secretary of War Jefferson Davis accepts Grant's resignation effective July 31, 1854.

June 13   Grant's ship, the *Sierra Nevada* stands off San Juan del Sur, Nicaragua.

June 17   He departs from Nicaragua to New York City on the *Prometheus*.

June 25   Grant arrives in New York City.

July   Ulysses visits with his parents in Bethel, Ohio.

August   Ulysses S. Grant is home in Missouri.

Bibliography
and Index

Selected Bibliography

In order to keep this bibliography within useful bounds, many of the standard and well-known Grant references which were consulted in the preparation of this book have not been included. With a few exceptions, this bibliography records material specifically useful to the storyline of this work.

Adams, Kramer A. *Covered Bridges of the West.* Berkeley, Calif.: Howell-North, 1963.

Anderson, C.L.G. *Old Panama.* New York: North River Press, 1938.

Arnold, Matthew. *General Grant With A Rejoinder By Mark Twain.* Carbondale: Southern Illinois Univ. Press, 1966.

Arthur, Louis A., ed. *Eunice Tripler: Some Notes of Her Personal Recollections.* New York: The Grafton Press, 1910.

Autenrieth, E.L. *Isthmus of Panama.* New York: J.H. Colton, 1851.

Avery, Mary W. *Washington: A History of the Evergreen State.* Seattle: Univ. of Washington Press, 1961.

Beebe, Lucius and Charles Clegg. *San Francisco's Golden Era.* Berkeley: Howell-North, 1960.

Belfords, Clarke & Co. *General Grant Abroad.* Chicago: Belfords, Clark & Co., 1879.

Billington, Ray Allen. *The Far Western Frontier 1830-1860.* New York: Harper & Brothers, 1956.

—————. *The Genesis of the Frontier Thesis.* San Marino: The Huntington Library, 1971.

Brotherton, I.N. "Jack." *Annals of Stanislaus County.* Vol. 1. Santa Cruz, Calif.: Western Tanager Press, 1982.

Bryan, James William, ed. *The Grant Memorial in Washington.* Washington: Government Printing Office, 1924.

Burt, Olive W. *The Story of American Railroads.* New York: The John Day Co., 1965.

Cadwaller, Sylvanus. *Three Years With Grant.* New York: Alfred A. Knopf, 1956.

California. *Fort Humboldt State Historic Park.* Sacramento: Department of Parks and Recreation, Jan., 1974.

_____ *Fort Humboldt State Historical Park; Preliminary General Development Plan.* Sacramento: Department of Parks and Recreation, Nov., 1977.

Camp, William Martin. *San Francisco, Port of Gold.* Garden City, New York: Doubleday & Company Inc., 1947.

Carpenter, Allan and Tom Balow. *Nicaragua.* Chicago: Children's Press, 1971.

Catton, Bruce. *The Army of the Potomac: Mr. Lincoln's Army.* Garden City: Doubleday & Co., Inc., 1951.

_____ *The Army of the Potomac: Glory Road.* Garden City: Doubleday & Company, Inc., 1952.

_____ *The Army of the Potomac: A Stillness at Appomattox.* Garden City: Doubleday & Co., Inc., 1953.

_____ *U. S. Grant and The American Military Tradition.* New York: Grosset & Dunlap, 1954.

_____ *This Hallowed Ground.* New York: Doubleday & Co., Inc., 1956.

_____ *America Goes to War.* Middletown, Connecticut: Wesleyan Univ. Press, 1958.

_____ *Grant Moves South.* Boston: Little, Brown and Co., 1960.

_____ *Grant Takes Command.* Boston: Little, Brown and Co., 1968.

_____, ed. "Grant Writes Home." *American Heritage,* Oct., 1973.

_____ *Reflections on the Civil War.* New York: Doubleday & Co., Inc., 1981.

"Chargres River Route to California in 1851." *Quarterly of the California Historical Society.* Vol. VIII. No. 1 Mar., 1929.

Childs, George W. *Recollections of General Grant.* Philadelphia: Collins Printing House, 1890.

Church, William Conant. *Ulysses S. Grant.* New York: G. P. Putnam's Sons, 1897.

Cleland, Robert Glass. *A History of California: The American Period.* New York: The Macmillan Company, 1923.

Cowell, Josephine W. *History of Benicia Arsenal.* Berkeley, Howell-North Press, 1963.

Coy, Owen Cochran. *The Humboldt Bay Region, 1850-1875.* Los Angeles: The California State Historical Association, 1929.

Criswell, John F. *Knight's Ferry's Golden Past.* Oakdale, California: by the Author, 1972.

Curtis, David. "Early Failure of a Conquering Hero." *The Pacific Historian.* Winter, 1975.

Edwards, Malcolm. *The California Diary of General E. D. Townsend.* The Ward Ritchie Press, 1970.

Elderkin, James D. *Biographical Sketches and Anecdotes.* Detroit: 1899.

Elliott, Wallace W. *History of Humboldt County.* San Francisco: Wallace W. Elliott & Co., 1881.

Emparan, Madie Brown. *The Vallejos of California.* San Francisco: The Gleeson Library Associates, 1968.

Fabens, Joseph W. *Life on the Isthmus.* New York: George P. Putnam & Co. 1853.

Ferris, S. C. "Hardships of the Isthmus in '49." *The Century Magazine.* Apr., 1891.

Folkman, David I., Jr. *The Nicaragua Route.* Salt Lake City: Univ. of Utah Press, 1972.

Forbes-Lindsay, C. H. *Panama: The Isthmus and the Canal.* Philadelphia: The John C. Winston Co., 1906.

"Fort Vancouver National Historical Site." Wash., D.C. *National Park Service,* 1978.

Fountain, Susie Baker. Vol. 32 of her Papers. Humboldt State Univ. Library, Arcata, Calif., 1967.

Fourth U. S. Infantry Regiment. *Day Book of Company A: 1848-1853.*

Fraser, J. P. Munro., ed. *History of Solano County*. San Francisco: Wood Alley & Co., 1879.

Frazer, Robert W., ed. *Joseph K. F. Mansfield on the Conditions of the Western Forts, 1853-1854*. Norman: Univ. of Oklahoma Press. 1963.

_____. *Forts of the West*. Norman: Univ. of Oklahoma Press, 1965.

Frost, Lawrence A. *U. S. Grant Album*. Seattle: Superior Publishing Co., 1966.

Garland, Hamlin. "Grant's Quiet Years at Northern Posts." *McClure's Magazine*. Mar. 1, 1897.

_____. *Ulysses S. Grant: His Life and Character*. New York: The Macmillan Company, 1920.

Genzoli, Andrew M. *Redwood Country*. Eureka: Schooner Features, 1973.

Giberson, N. S. "Captain Grant's Old Post, Fort Humboldt." *The Overland Monthly* Vol. 8, Second Series, 1886.

Gillogly, Clarabelle Haven. "Vancouver Barracks as Remembered." *Fort Vancouver Historical Society*, 1964.

Goetzmann, William H. *Army Exploration in the American West: 1803-1863*. New Haven: Yale Univ. Press, 1950.

Goldhurst, Richard. *Many Are The Hearts: The Agony and Triumph of Ulysses S. Grant*. New York: Reader's Digest Press, 1975.

Grant, Jesse R. *In the Days of My Father General Grant*. New York: Harper & Brothers, 1925.

Grant, U. S. *Personal Memoirs of U. S. Grant*. 2 vols. New York: Charles L. Webster & Company, 1885.

_____. *Account Book, 1839-1843*, in the Huntington Library, San Marino. Calif.

Grant, U. S. 3rd. *Ulysses S. Grant: Warrior and Statesman*. New York: William Morrow & Company, Inc., 1969.

Gray, S. C. *History of Solano County*. San Francisco: Wood, Alley & Co., 1879.

Gregory, Thomas Jefferson. *History of Solano and Napa Counties*. Los Angeles: Historic Record Co., 1912.

Griswold, Chauncey D. *The Isthmus of Panama*. New York: Dewitt and Devenport, 1852.

Gudde, Erwin G. and Elisabeth K. Gudde, eds. *California Gold Camps*. Berkeley: Univ. of California Press, 1975.

Guinn, James Miller. *History of the State of California and Biographical Record of the San Joaquin Valley*. Chicago: The Chapman Publishing Co., 1905.

Hart, Herbert M. *Old Forts of the Northwest*. Seattle: Superior Publishing Co., 1963.

_____ *Old Forts of the Southwest*. Seattle: Superior Publishing Co., 1964.

_____ *Old Forts of the Far West*. Seattle: Superior Publishing Co., 1965.

Headley, J. T. *The Life and Travels of General Grant*. Philadelphia: Hubbard Bros., 1879.

_____ *The Travels of General Grant*. Philadelphia: New World Publishing Co., 1881.

Heizer, Robert F. ed. *Handbook of North American Indians*. Vol. 8. Wash., D. C.: Smithsonian Institution, 1978.

Hine, Robert F. and Savoie Lottinville. *Soldier in the West: Letters of Theodore Talbot During His Services in California, Mexico, and Oregon, 1845-53*. Norman: Univ. of Oklahoma Press, 1972.

Hittell, Theodore H. *History of California*. Vols 2 and 3. San Francisco: N. J. Stone & Company, 1898.

Holbrook, Stewart H. *The Columbia*. New York: Holt, Rinehart and Winston, 1974.

Hoopes, Chad L. *Lure of Humboldt Bay Region*. Dubuque, Iowa: Kendall/Hunt Publishing Co., 1971.

_____ *Fort Humboldt*. Master's Thesis, Brigham Young Univ., Provo, Utah, 1963.

Hoover, Mildred Brooke; Eugene Hero Rensch; and Ethel Grace Rensch, *Historic Spots in California*. Stanford: Stanford Univ. Press, 1948.

Howarth, David. *Panama*. New York: McGraw-Hill, 1966.

Hubbard, Harry D. *Vallejo*. Boston: Meador Publishing, 1941.

Hunt, Marguerite. *History of Solano County*. Vol. 1. Chicago: S. J. Clarke Publishing Co., 1926.

Hunt, Rockwell D. *California Pioneers I Have Known*. Stockton: Univ. of the Pacific, 1962.

Hussey, John A. *The History of Fort Vancouver*. Portland: Abbot, Kerns & Bell Co., 1957.

Hussey, Roland Dennis. *Spanish Colonial Trails in Panama*. Mexico: Panamerican Institute of Geography and History, 1939.

Irvine, Leigh H. *History of Humboldt County California.* Los Angeles: Historic Record Co., 1915.

Irving, Washington. *Adventures of Captain Bonneville.* Portland, Oregon: Binfords & Mort, 1954.

Jacobson, Pauline. *City of the Golden 'Fifties.* Berkeley: Univ. of Calif. Press, 1941.

Jones, Idwal. "A Captain at Fort Humboldt." *Westways,* Jan., 1949.

_____. "Dining with Captain Grant." *Gourmet,* Nov., 1951.

_____. *Ark of Empire.* New York: Doubleday & Co., Inc., 1951.

Kemble, John Haskell. "Pacific Mail Service Between Panama and San Francisco, 1849-1851." *The Pacific Historical Review,* Dec., 1933.

_____. "The Panama Route to the Pacific Coast, 1848-1869." *The Pacific Historical Review,* Mar., 1938.

_____. *The Panama Route, 1848-1869.* Berkeley: Univ. of Calif. Press, 1943.

_____, ed. *Gold Rush Steamers.* San Francisco: The Book Club of California, 1958.

_____, ed. *The Panama Canal: The Evolution of the Isthmian Crossing.* San Francisco: The Book Club of California, 1965.

Kirkpatrick, R. Z. "General Grant in Panama." *The Military Engineer.* Vol. XXVI. No. 146 Mar.-Apr., 1934.

Larke, J. K., and J. Harris Patton. *General U. S. Grant: His Early Life and Military Career.* New York: Thomas Kelly, 1885.

Lavine, Harold. *Central America.* New York: Time Inc., 1964.

Leeper, David Rohrer. *The Argonauts of 'Forty-Nine.* Columbus, Ohio: Long's College Book Co., 1950. (Reprint).

Letts, J. M. *A Pictoral View of California; Including a Description of The Panama and Nicaragua Routes.* New York: Henry Bill, 1853.

Lewis, Lloyd. *Captain Sam Grant.* Boston: Little, Brown and Co., 1950.

_____. *Letters from Lloyd Lewis.* Boston: Little, Brown and Co., 1950.

Lewis, Oscar. *The Quest for Qual-A-Wa-Loo (Humboldt Bay).* San Francisco, 1943.

_____, ed. *Sea Routes to the Gold Fields in 1849-1852.* New York: Alfred A. Knopf, 1949.

Lewis, Oscar. *This Was San Francisco.* New York: David McKay Co., Inc. 1962.

Lewis, William S., ed. *Reminiscences of Delia B. Sheffield.* Seattle: Univ. of Wash. Press, 1924.

Leyden, James A. *A Historical Sketch of the Fourth Infantry.* Fort Sherman, Idaho: Press of the Fourth United States Infantry, 1891.

Long, E. B., ed. *Personal Memoirs of U. S. Grant.* Cleveland and New York: The World Publishing Co., 1952.

Lotchin, Robert W. *San Francisco 1846-1856 from Hamlet to City.* New York: Oxford Univ. Press, 1974.

Martin, V. Covert. *Stockton Album: Through the Years.* Stockton, Calif.: Simard Printing Co., 1959.

McCullough, David. *The Path Between the Seas.* New York: Simon and Schuster, 1977.

McFeely, William S. *Grant: A Biography.* New York: W. W. Norton & Co., 1981.

McKittrick, Myrtle M. *Vallejo, Son of California.* Portland: Binfords & Mort, 1944.

Meredith, Roy. *Mr. Lincoln's General, U. S. Grant.* New York: E. P. Dutton and Company, Inc., 1959.

Meyer, Howard N. *Let Us Have Peace: The Story of Ulysses S. Grant.* New York: Collier Books, London: Collier-Macmillan Ltd., 1966.

Minter, John Easter. *The Chagres.* New York: Rinehart & Co., Inc., 1948.

Muscatine, Doris. *Old San Francisco.* New York: G. P. Putnam's Sons, 1975.

Nixon, Stuart. *Redwood Empire.* New York: E. P. Dutton & Co., Inc., 1966.

Otis, Fessenden Nott. *Illustrated History of the Panama Railroad.* New York: Harper & Brothers, 1862.

Overmeyer, George W. "George B. McClellan and the Pacific Northwest." *Pacific Northwest Quarterly.* Jan., 1941.

Paden, Irene D. and Margaret E. Schlichtmann. *The Big Oak Flat Road.* San Francisco: Lawton Kennedy, 1955.

Palmer, Loomis T. (L. P. Remlap). *General U. S. Grant's Tour Around the World.* Chicago: J. Fairbanks & Co., 1885.

Parmelee, Robert D. *Pioneer Sonoma.* Sonoma, California, The Sonoma Index-Tribune, 1972.

Pitkin, Thomas M. *Grant The Soldier*. Washington: Acropolis Books, 1965.

——————. *The Captain Departs*. Carbondale: Southern Illinois Univ. Press, 1973.

Pitt, Leonard. *The Decline of the Californios*. Berkeley: Univ. of Calif. Press, 1966.

Post, James L., compiler. *Reminiscences by Personal Friends of Gen. U.S. Grant and the History of Grant's Log Cabin*. St. Louis: By the Author, 1904.

Powell, William H. *A History of the Fourth Regiment of Infantry*. Washington: M'Gill & Witherow, 1871.

Powers, Alfred. *Redwood Country*. New York: Duell, Sloan & Pearce, 1949.

Pratt, Julius H. "To California By Panama in '49." *The Century Magazine*. Apr., 1891.

Prosch, Thomas W. "The United States Army in Washington Territory." *Washington Historical Quarterly*. Oct., 1907.

Read, Georgia Willa. "The Chagres River Route to California in 1851." *Quarterly of the California Historical Society*, Mar., 1929.

Rolle, Andrew F. *California: A History*. New York: Thomas Y. Crowell Co., 1969.

Roske, Ralph J. *Everyman's Eden, A History of California*. New York: The Macmillan Co., 1968.

Ross, Ishbel. *The General's Wife: the Life of Mrs. Ulysses S. Grant*. New York: Dodd, Mead & Co., 1959.

"Saga of Sonoma." *Sonoma Valley Historical Society*, Sonoma, Calif., 1976.

Schmitt, Martin F., ed. *General George Crook: His Autobiography*. Norman: Univ. of Oklahoma Press, 1946.

Seifert, Shirley. *Captain Grant*. Philadelphia: J. B. Lippincott Co., 1946.

Sheldon, Henry I. *Nicaragua Canal*. Chicago: A. C. McClurg & Co., 1902.

Sherman, William T. *Recollections of California*. Oakland: Biobooks, 1945.

——————. *Memoirs* Vol. 1. New York: D. Appleton and Co., 1875.

Shields, Clara M. George. "General Grant at Fort Humboldt in The Early Days." *Humboldt Times*, Eureka, Calif., Nov. 10, 1912.

Simon, John Y. *Ulysses S. Grant Chronology.* Athens, Ohio: The Ohio Historical Soc., 1963.

_____, ed. *The Papers of Ulysses S. Grant,* 14 vols. Carbondale: Southern Illinois Univ. Press, 1967-1985.

_____ "The Rediscovery of Ulysses S. Grant." *Inland: The Magazine of the Middle West.* Jan., 1974.

Smith, Joe. "U. S. Grant, Black Bart, and the Covered Bridges." *Ford Times,* Sept., 1958.

Solano County Historical Society. *Benicia's Early Glory, 1853-1854.* Benicia, Calif., 1958.

Starr, Kevin. *Americans and the California Dream: 1850-1915.* New York: Oxford Univ. Press, 1973.

Stickles, Arndt M. *Simon Bolivar Buckner.* Chapel Hill: The Univ. of North Carolina Press, 1940.

Strong, James C. "Reminiscences of a Pioneer of the Territory of Washington." *The Washington Historical Quarterly,* July 1912.

Tebbel, John. *The Compact History of the Indian Wars.* New York: Hawthorn Books, Inc., 1966.

Thornbury, D. L. *California's Redwood Wonderland.* San Francisco: Sunset Press, 1923.

Tinkham, George H. *A History of Stockton.* San Francisco: W. M. Hinton & Co., 1880.

_____ *History of Stanislaus County.* Los Angeles: Historic Record Co., 1921.

Todd, Helen. *A Man Named Grant.* Boston: Houghton Mifflin Co., 1940.

Travers, James W. *California.* Los Angeles: Wetzel Publishing Co., Inc., 1950.

Tripler, Eunice. *Some Notes of Her Personal Recollections.* New York: The Grafton Press, 1910.

Utley, Robert M. *Frontiersmen in Blue, The United States Army and the Indian 1848-1865.* New York: The Macmillan Co., 1967.

Van Arsdol, Ted. "History of the 14th Infantry." *Clark County History.* 1971.

Van Sicklen, Helen Putnam. "The Life and Times of General M. G. Vallejo." *Quarterly of the Society of California Pioneers.* San Francisco: Sept., 1932.

Washington, *The Official History of the Washington National Guard: Heritage of the Washington Territorial Militia.* Tacoma: Office of the Adjutant General, 1961.

Watkins, T. H. *California, An Illustrated History.* Palo Alto: American West Publishing Co., 1973.

Whiting, J. S. *Forts of the State of Washington.* Seattle: by the Author, 1951.

Williams, Kenneth P. *Lincoln Finds a General.* New York: The Macmillan Co., 1952.

Williams, T. Harry. *Lincoln and His Generals.* New York: Alfred A. Knopf, 1952.

Wilson, Edmund. *Patriotic Gore: Studies in the Literature of the American Civil War.* New York: Oxford Univ. Press, 1962.

Wilson, James Grant. *Life and Public Services of General Ulysses S. Grant.* New York: DeWitt, 1885.

_____. *General Grant.* New York: D. Appleton and Co., 1897.

Woodruff, Jacqueline McCart. *Benicia, The Promise of California.* Vallejo: By the Author, 1947.

Woodward, W. E. *Meet General Grant.* New York: Horace Liveright, 1928.

Woodward, William, and David Hansen, eds. *Military Influences on Washington History.* Tacoma: Washington Army National Guard, 1984.

Young, John Russell. *Around the World with General Grant.* New York: The American News Co., 1879.

Newspapers

Alta California	San Francisco, California
Blue Lake Advocate	Blue Lake, California
Christian Science Monitor	Boston, Massachusetts
Daily Evening Herald	Stockton, California
Daily Journal	Dayton, Ohio
Daily Territorial Enterprise	Virginia City, Nevada
Great Falls Tribune	Great Falls, Montana
Humboldt Standard	Eureka, California
Humboldt Times	Eureka, California
National Republican	Washington, D. C.
New York Herald Tribune	New York, New York

New York Sun   New York, New York
New York Times   New York, New York
New York World   New York, New York
Oregonian   Portland, Oregon
Panama Star and Herald   Panama City, Panama
Post Enquirer   Oakland, California
San Francisco Examiner   San Francisco, California
San Francisco Herald   San Francisco, California
San Joaquin Republican   Stockton, California
Stockton Argus   Stockton, California
West Coast Signal   Eureka, California

Index